The Story of Mary, Mother of Love

The Presence of Mary in the Life of Jesus

by

E. Mary Christie

Mother's House Publishing

Content of this book is the personal revelation of the author and is shared with the intent to acquaint the reader with the Blessed Mother of God through that revelation. No professional spiritual direction is intended nor implied.

Scriptural references are from The Latin Vulgate Douay-Rheims Catholic Bible (Biblia Sacra Vulgata). *Please note that the* Biblia Sacra Vulgata *originated about the year 382 A.D. when Pope Damasus commissioned St. Jerome to translate the original Greek and Hebrew texts into Latin. Author has substituted selected personal pronouns (thee, thou, thine) with modern versions for ease in reading and understanding. In all other respects, text quoted from the Douay-Rheims Catholic Bible remains as set forth herein.*

"Rescript" is a term currently in use for the former term "Imprimatur".

RESCRIPT

In accord with canon 827 of the Code of Canon Law, I hereby grant my permission to publish "The Story of Mary – Mother of Love," by E. Mary Christie.

Most Reverend Michael J. Sheridan
Bishop of Colorado Springs
Colorado Springs, Colorado
February 27, 2009

Published by
Mother's House Publishing
2814 East Woodmen Road
Colorado Springs, CO 80920
719-266-0437 / 800-266-0999
info@mothershousepublishing.com
www.mothershousepublishing.com

Design and interior layout by Jacqueline Haag
Printed and bound in Colorado Springs, CO
Made in the United States of America

ISBN 0-9792704-9-9

THIS BOOK IS CONSECRATED TO

The Sacred Heart of Jesus in an effort to heal His poor wounded Heart, which has been pierced through our careless sinfulness and our lack of love and reverence shown to the Eternal Father

AND TO

The Immaculate Heart of Mary in an effort to console her and in reparation for the world's blasphemies and ingratitude to her gentle motherly heart.

* * * * *

*To my beloved husband and best friend
who brought the Blessed Virgin Mary into my life
and through her, helped me to find the true Peace of Christ.*

* * * *

John 1:1-14

In the beginning was the Word, and the Word was with God, and the Word was God. The same was in the beginning with God. All things were made by Him: and without Him was made nothing that was made. In Him was Life, and the Life was the Light of men. And the Light shineth in darkness, and the darkness did not comprehend it.

There was a man sent from God, whose name was John. This man came for a witness, to give testimony of the Light, that all men might believe through him. He was not the Light, but was to give testimony of the Light. That was the true Light, which enlighteneth every man that cometh into this world. He was in the world, and the world was made by Him, and the world knew Him not.

He came unto His own, and His own received Him not. But to as many as received Him, He gave them power to be made the sons of God, to them that believe in His name, who are born, not of blood, nor of the will of the flesh, nor of the will of man, but of God. And the Word was made flesh, and dwelt among us. And we saw His glory, the glory as of the Only-begotten of the Father, full of grace and truth.

Proverbs 8:22-35

The Lord possessed me in the beginning of His ways, before He made any thing from the beginning. I was set up from eternity, and of old before the earth was made. The depths were not as yet, and I was already conceived. Neither had the fountains of waters as yet sprung out. The mountains with their huge bulk had not as yet been established. Before the hills I was brought forth.

He had not yet made the earth, nor the rivers, nor the poles of the world. When He prepared the heavens, I was present; when with a certain law and compass He enclosed the depths; when He established the sky above, and poised the fountains of waters; when He compassed the sea with its bounds, and set a law to the waters that they should not pass their limits; when He balanced the foundations of the earth; I was with Him in His forming all things and was delighted every day, playing before Him at all times.

Playing in the world: and my delights were to be with the children of men. Now therefore, ye children, hear me: Blessed are they that keep my ways. Hear instruction and be wise, and refuse it not. Blessed is the man that heareth me, and that watcheth daily at my gates, and waiteth at the posts of my doors. He that shall find me, shall find life, and shall have salvation from the Lord:

Dear Reader:

May you find herein, an enjoyable tour of the four Gospels, written in a simple, easy-to-understand way, accenting on the important role the Mother of Jesus played in the life and times of the Incarnate Son of God, based on her complete trust and absolute devotion to the Father Almighty.

May the example of Mary's great love of God, her strength to face life's challenges through her indomitable faith in His Goodness and Mercy, her purity of heart that kept her always patient and kind, loving and forgiving, never spiteful or angry, her absolute selflessness that kept her free from self-indulgence, enviousness or boastfulness - inspire you to follow her holy example; and may you find herein a treasury of spiritual gifts to further assist and guide your pilgrimage along life's arduous journey toward Heaven, our eternal goal.

For the Reader will readily acknowledge that Mary, destined to bear God Incarnate in her virgin womb, had to be conceived without the stain of sin upon her soul. And being so pure of body, mind, heart and soul, she would have been as perfect a human being as could be found on the earth, as indeed all of God's graces were lavishly bestowed upon her – just as the angel Gabriel had greeted her, "Hail, full of Grace". It goes without saying that Mary's love for God was as pure as the driven snow; it would have glowed within her like an ever-burning fire, lighting up her countenance and shining through her eyes. Like her Divine Son, she would have radiated joy, peace and perfect charity so that all who came in contact with her would have enjoyed being in her presence; and like the blossoming of a rare and exquisite flower, all who perceived Mary would have remarked on her loveliness and readily recognized in her all the virtues of holiness.

May this tribute to the Blessed Virgin Mary, fire your imagination, dear Reader, so that you may more readily become caught up in the magic of those joyful and glorious mysteries to be marveled at - or share in the more emotional moments of those sorrowful mysteries surrounding the Passion, Crucifixion and Death of our loving Saviour, thereby encouraging you to meditation and a desire for contemplative prayer, and inspiring you to a deeper spiritual devotion to the one Eternal God – through the Immaculate Heart of Mary, blessed Daughter of the Eternal Father, Mother of the Son Incarnate, and Spouse most pure of the Holy Ghost.

Author

The Christian Story is a holy story. It invites fascination and awe, and thus has been told and retold countless times. As long as there will be human beings yearning for redeeming love, its fascination will not fade but perdure. And as long as people of good will are contemplating the grandeur of God become one of us, this Good News will be a truly awe-inspiring message. Who better than Mary to lead us into the depth of these fascinating and awesome mysteries? E. Mary Christie, drawing on biblical and apocryphal sources matured in personal meditation and reflection, tells us the story of this great woman whose one and only purpose in life was, and still is to lead us to her Son. Indeed, **The Story of Mary-Mother of Love**, is a contemplative narrative pondering the life of the Mother of Jesus Christ with both genuine fascination and awe.

Rev. Johann G. Roten, SM
Director
The Marian Library/International
Marian Research Institute
University of Dayton

Chapter 1

The Annunciation

Upon her knees, the young Virgin was praying. In the gentle darkness, through the narrow window of that humble room, the softened moonlight cast its ethereal glow over her serene and lovely face, composed in joyful ecstasy. A peaceful quietude pervaded the tiny chamber.

Dimly she became aware of a suffusion of light that steadily filled the room with its intensity. Mary opened her eyes and perceived in wonder the apparent object of luminosity – the figure of an angelic being, his face ineffably beautiful, his eyes aflame; he was on bended knee before her, his hand raised in greeting: *"Hail, full of Grace, the Lord is with thee! Blessed art thou among women!"*[1]

Overwhelmed by this salutation, Mary stared in trembling fascination at the presence before her, her eyes wide with astonishment. What manner of greeting was this! She could feel her heart glowing in the presence of this celestial being, whom she immediately recognized to be a Messenger of God the Most High.[2] *"Do not be afraid, Mary, for you have found favour with God,"*[3] the soft, angelic voice addressed her consternation. *"You will conceive and bear a Son, and you will name Him Jesus. He shall be great and will be called the Son of the Most High. And the Lord God will give to Him the throne of His ancestor David. He will reign over the house of Jacob for ever and of His Kingdom there shall be no end."*[4]

At these words, the gentle Virgin bowed her head in deep humility; her mind in a turmoil. The words of the Messenger rang through her head in unbelievable amazement. From the

---

[1] Luke 1:28
[2] Luke 1:26
[3] Luke 1:30
[4] Luke 1:31-33

1

holy Scriptures she had not only known of, but in her great love for God, had longed for the coming of the Messiah, the Son of God who would come to redeem the world. From her earliest childhood she had inspired those around her with the intensity of her spiritual devotion and her complete faith in all that the prophets had imparted, her quiet passion filling her soul with a supernatural joy that radiated all about her.

As if one in a dreamlike state, she now stammered, *"How can this be since I know not man?"*[5] But Gabriel, the Archangel, answered her, *"The Holy Ghost will come upon you and the power of the Most High will overshadow you. And therefore the Child to be born will be holy; He will be called the Son of God,"* and addressing Mary's awed speechlessness, he continued, *"And now your cousin Elizabeth in her old age has also conceived a son; and this is the sixth month for her who was said to be barren: for nothing is impossible with God."*[6]

In the momentary silence that filled the tiny room, Mary's heart surged with a joy that knew no bounds as the full meaning of the angel's message slowly impinged itself upon her soul. Without further hesitation, the lowly Maiden softly acquiesced: *"Behold the handmaid of the Lord; let it be done unto me according to thy Word."*[7]

Gabriel then departed,[8] leaving the room in complete darkness. But Mary's heart was aglow with a fire of intense love for her God. Her unhesitating Yes to the angel's revelation of God's plan of salvation was born out of her great love that had become such an integral part of her entire being; at the Archangel's bidding, to become the Mother of the Messiah dawned upon her soul as the most natural and complete progression of her purpose in life. Thus, totally humbled by the

---

[5] Luke 1:34
[6] Luke 1:35-37
[7] Luke 1:38
[8] Luke 1:38

great honour of such a precious Gift, she had willingly responded with absolute faith in the Word of God and complete trust in His holy Will, even knowing as she did from her biblical learning, that Christ, the promised Redeemer, now to be born into the world as her Incarnate Son, would suffer terribly to atone for the world's sinfulness.[9]

At Gabriel's departure, Mary fell into a deep prayer, the prayer of enraptured ecstasy, so utterly overcome and overjoyed was she in her great love for God.

And so it was that night, in the quietude of that meager chamber, at Mary's *Fiat,* the awesome power of the Holy Ghost overshadowed the lowly Maiden and she miraculously conceived the Christ Child in her virgin womb.

Dear Mother, most Lowly and Blessed,
May I be inspired and guided by your holy example of Humility
and by your complete Faith in the Word of God.

---

[9] Psalm 21:18-19; Isaias 50:6; Acts 3:18

Chapter 2

The Visitation

When the first rays of the Nazarene dawn suffused the heavens with pink splendour, it was to find the humble Virgin again on her knees in devout prayer. Through the narrow window of that tiny, sparsely furnished chamber, they steadily cast their golden glow over the lowly Maiden lost in ecstasy, lighting up her delicate and lovely features.

Mary remained in blissful rapture until the hour of the usual early morning Matins in the local synagogue. All who perceived her that morning were struck by her apparent radiance, her dark luminous eyes filled with an ecstatic joyfulness.

Mary then returned home to gently break the news of the angel's visit to her elderly father Joachim, humbly affirming her absolute belief in the miraculous Incarnation; she must leave at once to visit cousin Elizabeth, now in her sixth month with child as told by the Archangel Gabriel. From her knowledge of the Scriptures, Mary knew her cousin's child to be the one spoken of by the prophet, Isaias, *the voice of one crying in the wilderness* heralding the coming of the Messiah, the holy Child within her womb.[1] Without hesitation Mary's heart reached out to Elizabeth, determining that such a visit was not only imperative but also, she felt certain, her elderly cousin would need assistance; she would leave at first light the next morning.

Tenderly, Mary and Joachim held to each other, Joachim over-awed by the revelation yet humbled by the knowledge of this great Gift bestowed upon his only child. He accepted the news with complete faith and humility. He and his wife Anne (said to have died when Mary was very young), had known their daughter to be a special child of God, conceived as Mary was in

---

[1] Matt. 3:3

their old age in answer to their prayers, and indeed they had offered their baby daughter to God in the Temple at Jerusalem in loving thanksgiving. As the child grew they had readily noticed Mary's insatiable yearning to learn more of God and all the biblical teachings; she would plead with her parents to be left in the Temple, where her tiny form would frequently be found on both knees, lost in prayer. Thus it was, from the tender age of three, Mary gave her service to the Temple, in loving submission to God's holy Will. All who knew Mary recognized in her a great supernatural love of God, which infused charity and joyfulness amazed and inspired all those around her. That she was with purity of body, heart, mind, and soul remained an indisputable fact as she grew into young adolescence and adulthood.

Quickly Mary made preparations for her long journey to the city of Juda[2] and at first light she joined a small caravan departing Nazareth for the hilly region. It was a slow and arduous progress on foot, the terrain steeply undulating, harsh and unforgiving. During the day, the sun appeared a relentless scorching ball in the heavens, disappearing over the horizon in the early evening and taking with it the intensity of its heat, leaving a cold, damp, darkness in its wake. By dawn on their last day, the travelers were happy to note the distant white rooftops of the city's dwellings.

Once inside the gates of Juda, Mary broke away from her traveling companions to seek out the house of Elizabeth and Zachary.[3] On entering its courtyard, she perceived her elderly cousin Elizabeth seated on a low stone wall surrounding the water-well, splashing her face with its icy coolness in the early heat of the day. Softly the gentle Maiden approached.

At her salutation, Elizabeth rose in wonder – for at the sound of Mary's greeting, the child in Elizabeth's womb leapt for joy[4] and in that moment, the Visitation of the unborn Christ

---

[2] Luke 1:39
[3] Luke 1:5-7; Luke 1:40
[4] Luke 1:41

Child and His sanctification of the baby she was soon to deliver, were revealed to her. As the cousins clasped each other in excitement, the older woman cried out with elation at her wondrous revelation, "*Blessed art thou among women, and blessed is the fruit of thy womb! How is this happening to me, that the mother of my Lord should come to me? For as soon as I heard your greeting, the infant in my womb leaped for joy. Blessed are you who believed; for because of your great faith, those things will be accomplished that were spoken to you by the Lord.*"[5]

Mary's face resounded her absolute joy, and with eyes cast Heavenward, she replied, "*My soul magnifies the Lord and my spirit rejoices in God my Saviour. For He has looked upon the humility of His handmaid and from henceforth all generations shall call me blessed because He that is mighty has done great things to me. Holy is His name; and His mercy shall flow from generation to generations, to all those who fear Him.*"[6]

Then, tenderly, she took Elizabeth's hands and looking deep into the gentle eyes before her, she shared her profound knowledge of God's prophetic plan of salvation for mankind: "*He has shown might in His arm: He has scattered the proud in the conceit of their heart; He has put down the mighty from their high seat, and has exalted the humble; He has filled the hungry with good things, and the rich He has sent away empty-handed; and being infinitely merciful He has received His people Israel as His servants: as He did speak to our fathers, to Abraham, and to Abraham's seed for ever.*"[7]

What an amazing canticle from the heart of this pure and lowly Maiden standing before Elizabeth. Mary and her cousin

---

[5] Luke 1:42-45
[6] Luke 1:46-50
[7] Luke 1:51-55

stared at each other, their eyes shining with an ecstatic joyfulness, yet both overcome with a deepened sense of profound humility. Silently, arm-in-arm, they turned away from the well and walked slowly into the house of Zachary and Elizabeth.

The days that followed were spent in joyful preparation as the cousins worked together, giving thanks to Almighty God throughout their busy day in prayerful supplications and songs of praise. Both were aware of the exceptional bond that would exist between their yet unborn infants - the prophetic introduction of God's salvation to the world that the birth of Elizabeth's child would announce, and that the birth of Mary's Christ Child would invoke.

In the quiet of the evening, Elizabeth shared with Mary the day of Zachary's appointment with the Archangel Gabriel,[8] who had also appeared to her husband while he was alone offering incense in the Temple to God according to the custom of his priestly office.[9] The angel had announced that Elizabeth, though barren, would bear a son in her advanced years – astounding news which Zachary had found difficulty in believing. Gabriel had then gone on to announce that Zachary would be made dumb from the moment of his disbelief until the birth of his prophesied child.[10] And indeed, as Mary had readily noticed, Zachary had been unable to utter a single word since her arrival.

Mary spent three joyous months in the house of Elizabeth and Zachary,[11] when finally Elizabeth gave birth to her son.[12] What joy to behold the newborn infant! What happy pleasure in working together to tender his every waking need. What cherished moments as Mary, Elizabeth and Zachary would

---

[8] Luke 1:11
[9] Luke 1:9
[10] Luke 1:18-20
[11] Luke 1:56
[12] Luke 1:57

watch the treasured infant, relishing in his tiny features so peacefully tranquil as he lay sleeping in their arms. This precious baby - who would grow into manhood and herald the coming of the Messiah.

When it came to the time for the child to be circumcised and named according to Jewish tradition (on the eighth day after birth), kinsfolk and neighbours assumed the child would be named Zachary after his father, but Elizabeth refused, saying the name of her child would be John.[13] All were surprised at her insistence. They turned to the silent father, and at Elizabeth's bidding, a writing tablet was hastily brought to him that he might make his own wishes made known. In bold letters, Zachary confirmed that their son's name would be JOHN. And at that moment, Zachary found his speech. Holding the baby high at arm's length so that all could see the child, he spoke out loud, giving praise and thanks to Almighty God,[14] *"Blessed be the Lord God of Israel; because He has come to save His people".*[15]

To the absolute amazement of all before him, he later prophesized, *"And you, child, will be called the prophet of the Highest, for you shall go before the face of the Lord to prepare His ways: to give knowledge of salvation to His people, to the remission of their sins; through the mercy of our God, in which the Orient from on High has visited us to enlighten those who sit in darkness; and in the shadow of death to direct our feet into the ways of righteousness and in peace".*[16]

What prophetic words to astound the crowds, who had quickly pressed closer in their eagerness to hear the hitherto silent Zachary. And Mary, in silent appreciation, with great love

---

[13] Luke 1:59-61
[14] Luke 1:62-64
[15] Luke 1:68
[16] Luke 1:76-79

and tenderness, watched all that passed before her, pondering and treasuring all these things in her heart.

The Feast of the Circumcision over, Mary then made preparations to leave Juda and return to her hometown of Nazareth.

Dear Mary, ever Caring and Selfless,
May I be inspired and guided by your holy example
to practice Charity and Unselfishness throughout my daily life.

Chapter 3

The Nativity

There was one, Joseph of the House of David, a devout man of God, both chaste and just, whom Joachim had determined to be a fitting guardian and protector for his young daughter. Mary and Joseph were thus betrothed in the days before the angel's Annunciation.

Before leaving the little town of Nazareth to visit her cousin Elizabeth, Mary had shared with Joseph the news of the Archangel's revelation and that she was now with Child. The older man wrestled over how best to deal with the situation - for their envisaged relationship was to remain a pure and chaste one, both Mary and Joseph having consecrated their purity to God; the obviousness of Mary's condition with Child might prove awkward before the eyes of those who knew nothing of the Miraculous Conception, and Joseph was therefore not willing to publicly expose his betrothed.[1]

In the days of Mary's absence, however, an angel of the Lord appeared to him while he slept, telling him to have no fear but to take Mary as his wife, affirming that the Child she had conceived was of the Holy Ghost,[2] and assuring him that all would be well.

So it was with great joy that Joseph greeted Mary on her arrival back home. In all humility he listened to Mary's humble recounting of the angel's visit to her announcing the Miraculous Conception of the Christ Child in her womb, and to her telling of Gabriel's visit to Zachary beforehand announcing the birth of a child who would herald the coming of the Messiah.

Over the months to follow, Mary and Joseph joyfully gave thanks to God, devoting much of their time in loving prayer. As

---

[1] Matt. 1:19
[2] Matt. 1:18

the ensuing days progressed, Mary grew in greater loveliness, her delicate features aglow with an ethereal radiance that shone with a supernatural joy and radiated a warmth and compassion that affected all around her. Family, friends, and acquaintances alike longed to be near her, relishing in the joy of her quiet presence.

When Mary was in her latter months with Child, news came to Nazareth that the ruling Caesar Augustus had decreed that all should be enrolled, each unto his own city. Mary and Joseph were both of the House of David, which would mean a 90-mile journey to the City of David, being Bethlehem in Judea.[3]

Together they made haste to prepare for the long journey. All around them others were busy preparing for their various journeys, the air charged with an air of excitement at the new challenges such a temporary migration would create. To those family members who were perhaps brought to the town of Nazareth in infancy or early childhood, such a crossing of the vast land on foot was a daunting prospect.

Although Mary had only months previously traveled back from far-away Juda, this new journey would provide a different challenge in her current physical condition; Joseph gave careful consideration to the route most likely to cause the least discomfort to Mary, and took pains to find a beast of burden with the least of dis-coordinated gaits.

In such biblical times, Jewish custom dictated that the man would be the one riding the donkey, his wife walking by his side, but Joseph, being a devout man and one without pride, insisted that Mary, bearing the Son of God in her virgin womb, should be the one to be mounted.

When at last all was made ready, Mary and Joseph set off in the early morning, anxious to get the most out of the first

---

[3] Luke 2:1-5

daylight hours before the sun would reach its zenith in all its scorching fury. They were not on the road long before they were passed by groups of travelers not hampered by the slow progress of a donkey, their happy chattering filling the air as they called to one another, the children squealing in the delight of their new venture.

The children would seem drawn to Mary and Joseph, looking up at Mary perched upon the donkey and noting the unusual loveliness of the gentle Maiden swathed in a pale blue handspun mantle, her golden hair just visible as it flowed in long tresses down her side. They would be caught by her gentle expression of love and joy as she smiled tenderly at them, her laughter that of pure delight as she watched their playful antics. Joseph too would be a source of grave interest, his tall figure striding manfully beside the donkey, an air of studious protectiveness as he guided the beast carefully along the roadway to avoid pitfalls and other objects in the way that might cause discomfort to his devoted charge.

The journey was a long and arduous one, stretching from one long, dusty, hot day into another, the evenings providing respite from the heat but a chilling coldness that did little to assuage the weary travelers of their discomfort. Although Mary and Joseph were no longer with the original set of travelers from Nazareth, they would be joined occasionally by others coming from other parts of the country, and would note passersby traveling in the opposite direction who were trying to reach Nazareth where they would need to be enrolled.

To Joseph and Mary, the distant sight of Bethlehem in the quiet of the late afternoon on their last day, came as a sweet relief. Even their weary donkey seemed to hasten his step. As the sun began its slow descent, the far away bright whites of the town's walls steadily became transformed into passive golds and oranges as the falling sun glistened back their mirage on the horizon. The desert sand sparkled with steadily darker shades of yellow and brown, and the stars of the oncoming night sky began to shine forth from an indigo blue as the day's end approached and their journey progressed to finality.

By the time Mary and Joseph reached the entrance to Bethlehem, it was to find a surprisingly intense hustle and bustle within. The narrow streets were crowded with an assortment of travellers, many carrying large pieces of luggage, others on camels or donkeys; men, women and children, all hurrying to find shelter for the night in the overly congested little town. In vain, Joseph sought to find accommodation. From one innkeeper to the next, he begged even the smallest of rooms; frantically he enquired of street vendors and passersby where he might find shelter for his wife now well advanced with child. But all to no avail. There simply was no room in that tiny, overcrowded place.

As the night progressed, and Joseph grew more weary, Mary gently consoled him, firm in her faith that a place would be found. As they rested by the local well for the coolness of its fresh water, an innkeeper's wife noted their plight, and approaching Joseph, she tentatively suggested that they might like to take shelter in a stable on the outskirts of the town where the local herdsmen would sometimes take their flock to rest for the night. Gratefully, Joseph embraced the idea.

The stable was surely a humble affair. There were a few beasts already housed within, looking up at Joseph with large limpid eyes as he made haste to clear an area for Mary to rest for the night. But the lowly refuge offered shelter from the cold night air and the kind innkeeper's wife had provided them with a small lamp, offering adequate lighting; there was plenty of fresh straw, sufficient to make a comfortable resting place, and Joseph went back out into the night to unload the donkey.

Mary opened her small bag of belongings to lay fresh linen cloths over the soft straw, and then she fell to her knees, giving thanks to Almighty God for all His blessings. Her heart, filled with gratitude, she fell into an ecstatic trance of joyous prayer.

When Joseph arrived back at the stable, armed with provisions, he surveyed the scene with absolute amazement. For, in that dimly lit stable, surrounded by cattle and sheep, upon a thick bed of soft straw, he perceived Mary on her knees in deep prayer, and lying beside her on the soft linen cloths, a beautiful newborn infant Child,[4] unclothed and spotlessly clean, His tiny fist wedged firmly in His little mouth as He noisily suckled and gurgled.

In an instant, Joseph fell to his knees beside the Infant just as Mary came out of her prayerful reverie. What overwhelming joy when they beheld the Incarnate Christ Child, miraculously delivered, as He had been miraculously conceived.[5]

With the tenderest of loving care, the Blessed Virgin gently wrapped the Babe in swaddling clothes and lifting Him into her arms, held Him close in abject adoration, all the while both Mary and Joseph filled with awesome wonder as the enormity of the wondrous Miracle before them blossomed to a complete dawning.

Quickly Joseph filled the stable's empty manger with fresh straw and soft linens, while Mary tendered to her Baby's newborn needs. And then they laid the sleeping baby Jesus in the manger and knelt at His side to adore Him, their hearts continuing to revel in the Miracle of the Godchild and giving praise and thanksgiving to Almighty God.

Without, the crisp night air was not only filled with the throbbing of insects and distant revelers, but also clear to Mary and Joseph, the sound of angelic voices singing hymns of praise and worship to the newborn King. Their joy was scarcely more

---

[4] Luke 2:6-7
[5] Matt. 1:23

than they could contain, their hearts bursting with a love that neither of them knew they could feel with such intensity. The presence of that one tiny Infant filled the humble stable with such a complete and absolute joy and peacefulness that even the cattle and sheep were silent.

Through the days that followed, Mary and Joseph watched adoringly over the Incarnate Child, marveling at the perfection of His tiny features composed in peaceful slumber or awake in animated wonder as His large blue eyes would look up into their adoring and doting faces.

And it came to pass, before Mary and Joseph left the stable with the baby Jesus, shepherds came from afar, gathering at the entrance of the tiny stall and begging sight of the Infant King. They had been watching their flock at night, they said, when an angel had appeared before them, brilliant as the brightest sunshine and radiant in his splendour. They had been sore afraid and could scarcely look at the presence before them, so awe-struck and filled with wonder were they. But the angel had calmed their mighty fear saying he had great tidings of joy – that a Child had been born in the City of David, *a Saviour, who is Christ the Lord,* and that a sign would be given to them, that they would find the Infant wrapped in swaddling clothes and lying in a manger. Earnestly and with great excitement, they reported that suddenly with the angel there appeared a multitude of heavenly beings praising God and singing *Glory to God in the highest; and on earth peace to men of good will.*[6]

Mary and Joseph, who had not been able to interrupt the shepherds' excitable recounting, promptly welcomed them into the lamplight of the stable. At the sight of the sleeping Infant lying in the manger, the humble herdsmen fell upon their knees in adoration, filled with awe and amazement. Tears streamed down their weather-beaten faces as the complete realization of the angel's message came fully home to their simple, humble

---

[6] Luke 2:9-14

minds. With one accord, they gave thanks to Almighty God and praised and adored the Christ Child.

And came too, other visitors to the manger to see the Babe in swaddling clothes; they were wise men from a-far, foreigners to the country, for, being astrologers and astronomers, they had seen the star at its rising which foretold the birth of the Messiah and had gone to King Herod to ask of him the whereabouts of the Infant King, feeling certain that he would have known of the birth. King Herod was troubled by their quest and gathered together all the chief priests and scribes to enquire where the Christ would be born. *"In Bethlehem of Judea"*, they had advised him, *"For so it is written by the prophet: And you Bethlehem in the land of Judea are not the least among the princes of Judea: for out of you will come forth a leader that will rule my people Israel"*. King Herod then told the wise men to search diligently for the Child and to bring back word to him of His whereabouts, so that he too could go and worship Him.[7]

So the Magi had sojourned to Bethlehem, following the single bright star in the East as it went before them, until it rested over the tiny stable. What joy when they entered and found the precious Babe lying in a manger. Falling on their knees, they worshipped the Infant King with much rejoicing.[8] Mary and Joseph were somewhat over-awed by their presence, their princely attire contrasting sharply with their own homespun clothing and humble surroundings. But the wise men seemed oblivious to all these things, intent only upon acknowledging Jesus as their King. With them they had brought Him gifts, and going out to their camels in the darkness, they brought back into the lamplight, their treasures of frankincense, gold and myrrh.[9]

---

[7] Matt. 2:1-8
[8] Matt. 2:9-11
[9] Matt. 2:11

Mary stared in wide-eyed wonder at what they laid before the Christ Child, it being instantly revealed to her that these were gifts of great symbolic significance: Frankincense for her Son's Divinity, Gold for His Kingship, Myrrh for His Humanity.

Dear Mother, Meek and Humble of heart,
May I be inspired and guided by your holy example
to pray for a detachment from the things of this world,
and aspire to Spiritual Poverty.

Chapter 4

The Presentation

On the eighth day after the birth of Jesus, Joseph took the baby Jesus to be circumcised according to Jewish custom, and that He might receive his official name, JESUS, as instructed by the angel Gabriel. The Blessed Virgin Mary, unable to attend at the Temple until after her Purification, remained alone at home, on her knees in the quiet of her small room, saddened over the prospect that her Divine Son would be shedding the first drops of His Most Precious Blood for mankind. Large tears spilled down her lovely face.

In these times, Jewish custom dictated that all women forty days after childbirth were to attend before a high priest for the Blessing of Purification before entering the Temple or partaking in any religious ceremonies. Mary, although she willingly obeyed the law, certainly did not require to be purified for she had remained pure even unto the birth of her Child. And indeed, having espoused herself to the Holy Ghost by her affirmative response to the holy messenger, she would inevitably remain faithful to her heavenly Spouse and chaste to the end of her days.

In obedience to the law therefore, on the fortieth day after the birth of Jesus, Mary and Joseph took their donkey and traveled the dusty, winding road from Bethlehem to Jerusalem for the ceremony of Mary's Purification - and to present the Christ Child in the Temple of Jerusalem in accordance with the law of Moses, handed down from God, that every first-born male child be called holy to the Lord and be presented to God before the Holy of Holies.[1]

---

[1] Luke 2:23

They left their gentle beast at the base of the Temple and tackled the lengthy flight of stone steps leading up to the great Gates of the magnificent structure, all the while careful not to disturb the sleeping baby Jesus in Mary's arms. Joseph carried the tiny cage bearing two turtledoves, being the minimum requirement under the law for Mary's Purification.

At the Temple Gates, Joseph surrendered the tiny cage and the high priest on duty gave Mary the necessary Blessing of Purification.

Once inside the edifice of splendid grandeur, Mary and Joseph made haste across the ornate flooring to join the small group of other families excitedly gathered in the massive hallways, awaiting their turn with the high priest. The Holy Family attracted a number of curious glances from the waiting group, who could not help noticing the loveliness of the fair young Maiden holding her angelic Baby with such tenderness and devotion, and the tall solid figure of Joseph, solicitous and attentive.

When finally it was the Holy Family's turn before the high priest, the Presentation of the Divine Son, in His humanity, to His Eternal Father in Heaven, filled both the Virgin Mary and her saintly spouse with an overwhelming depth of emotion. The gentle Mother looked down at the sleeping Son of the Most High, sacrificial Lamb of God, her heart overcome with an unspeakable grief.

As they slowly descended the steps leading from the entrance of the Holy of Holies - Joseph carefully shepherding Mary, now blinded by tears – their attention was suddenly diverted by an elderly man, determinedly shuffling his way toward them.

Simeon was his name, a just and devout prophet, who would not leave the Temple until he had cast his eyes upon the Saviour, *for the Holy Spirit was with him and he had great knowledge and wisdom.*[2] He begged to take the Child from Mary and gently holding Him in his elderly arms, he raised his eyes to Heaven and wept, *"Now you can dismiss your servant in peace, O Lord, according to your word; because my eyes have seen your Salvation which you have prepared before the face of all people: the Light of revelation for the Gentiles, and the glory of your people, Israel."*[3] What a bitter-sweet affirmation to Mary and Joseph's hearing!

Then, handing Jesus back to Mary, Simeon blessed God and spoke these words, *"Behold this Child is destined for the fall and the rise of many in Israel, and for a sign which shall be contradicted"* and looking intently into the eyes of the lowly Virgin before him, with a profound seriousness in his weathered countenance, he gently added, *"And your own soul a sword will pierce, that, out of many hearts, thoughts may be revealed."*[4]

A disturbing prophesy indeed. As the Blessed Mother held the baby Jesus close to her heart, the elderly prophet's words recalled Isaias' prediction and that which was written in the Book of Psalms that her Jesus would suffer terribly as the Redeemer, in His taking on the sins of the world in order to atone for our sinfulness.[5] Tenderly, Joseph led Mother and Child across the marbled floors of the great Temple, his own heart heavily burdened with sadness. Indeed, both Mary and Joseph would have cause to recall Simeon's prophecy over the many months and years to follow.[6]

Before they had reached the vast entranceway, they were greeted by yet another – a prophetess by the name of Anna. She was the daughter of Phanuel, of the tribe of Aser, and was also far advanced in years like Simeon. She had been a widow for a

---

[2] Luke 2:25-28
[3] Luke 2:29-32
[4] Luke 2:34-35
[5] Psalm 21:13-19; Isaias 50:6
[6] Luke 2:33

very long time, and would not leave the Temple but served there day and night, saying prayers and fasting. As she beheld the Holy Family, she instantly recognized the Christ Child - and to the amazement of all those gathered about her – she cried out that this was He who would be the Redeemer of Israel.[7]

Dear Mother, Mary Immaculate,
May I be inspired and guided by your holy example
to pray for the virtue of Purity.

---

[7] Luke 2:36-39

Chapter 5

Flight Into Egypt

Following the visit of the wise men to King Herod, the king waited anxiously for the return of the Magi. He had been troubled by the news of the newborn King,[1] fearing for his own kingship over all of Judea. But the days and months passed without word, for an angel had appeared to the wise men in a dream, advising them not to return to Herod but to take an alternative route back to their homes.[2]

Similarly Joseph too received a visit from an angel while he slept. He awoke troubled and alarmed, staring into the dark night as he collected his sleepy thoughts to make a plan of immediate action.

In the still of the night, the Blessed Virgin herself had been dozing on and off listening to the sound of her Baby's gentle breathing - so quiet, sometimes she was afraid He was not breathing at all. He was so tiny, so fragile, so precious. His small body, swathed in a handspun blanket, lay nestled in her arms.

But Mary's twilight state was aroused as Joseph's gentle voice broke the stillness, calling to her with an unexpected urgency in his tone. *"What is it, Joseph?"*. She lifted her head carefully so as not to disturb the precious bundle beside her. *"We must rise quickly and leave right away"*, he urged. Mary rose instantly, never doubting the instruction for a moment. Joseph immediately lit a candle and as they started gathering their few things together, he softly outlined the warning he had received from the angel - that they must leave Bethlehem

---

[1] Luke 2:3
[2] Luke 2:12

without delay, for King Herod was searching for the Christ Child with the intent to kill him.[3]

Suddenly Simeon's prophecy[4] tore at the Virgin's heartstrings - the thought of any harm coming to her baby Jesus was more than she could bear. It was like a knife searing into the very heart of her soul. Quickly she scooped the sleeping Child into her arms with a newfound terror. She pressed her gentle lips against His soft skin, smelling the sweet smell of her Infant King. Outside in the dim moonlight, Joseph was already loading the small donkey with his carpentry tools and their few personal possessions. As Mary took a last hurried look around the tiny room, a pang of sadness at leaving this, their first real home as the Holy Family, wrought a wistful look on her serene and lovely face.

Once out on the long road leading South of Bethlehem, Mary and Joseph moved swiftly but silently through the darkened night, their way lit only by the dim moonlight and the shining stars. Their small beast of burden plodded along with uneven gait, stalwartly bearing Mother and Child to safety. Joseph walked protectively beside the donkey, his staff gently swishing at the sand, his tall, cloaked figure a shadowy outline against the night sky. The baby Jesus did not stir, lying quietly in His loving Mother's gentle arms. All through the night the Holy Family traveled, the going rough and slow. They dared not stop to rest their weary limbs; Mary cold and cramped from her uncomfortable perch upon the donkey; Joseph, tired and foot-sore from his lengthy and tedious march through the ever-thickening sand.

Far above them, the vast night sky stretched into eternity, countless stars pin-pricking the darkness far and beyond. How small and vulnerable, that one small Family moving steadily across the barren wasteland, humbled by the stillness and deep

---

[3] Matt. 2:13-15
[4] Matt. 2:34-35

silence of the night and the grand majesty of that great emptiness. And yet didst the awesome Presence of the Eternal Father fall all about them, enshrouding them in a cloak of comforting protection.

Mary and Joseph remained silent as they trouped along, their hearts troubled by the prophetic threat to their precious baby Jesus. Surely even Herod would not wish to harm an innocent, helpless infant. And yet both could not forget the intent look in Simeon's aging eyes, nor the saddened ring to his words of prophetic doom.

Gradually the first rays of dawn infused their pink flush into the distant skyline, outlining strange and unusual shapes in a foreign landscape. Long would they journey across that unforgiving land, the road lengthy and arduous, the days hot and sweltering, the nights drawn-out and cold. *"Take the child to Egypt,"*[5] the angel had said. That alien land would become their new home, a haven of safety to nurture their tiny Infant into early childhood. A time of newfound challenges, of tears and laughter, newfound friendships and renewed joys. A time of sadness at leaving behind family and friends, the trials of finding acceptance amidst a foreign culture, the poverty that would inevitably accompany such a move.

And heartache. For quickly came the abominable news that King Herod, angry at not finding the baby Jesus, had ordered all infants under the age of two years throughout Bethlehem, killed.[6] Ah, what weeping and wailing throughout that land,[7] what unbearable heartache, inconsolable grieving. In the scorching heat of their new home, the Blessed Mother, holding Jesus, the Christ Child, close in her arms, fell to her knees in heart-wrenching, unspeakable sorrow.

---

[5] Matt. 2:13
[6] Matt. 2:16
[7] Matt. 2:17-18

Like a knife, ripping through the very depths of her soul, she felt the excruciating pain - and lamented bitterly over the loss of those innocent, precious, loved ones.

Dear Mother, most Obedient to the Will of God,
May I be inspired and guided by your holy example
to seek and accept God's holy Will throughout my life.

Chapter 6

The Finding of the Child Jesus in the Temple

The Holy Family remained in Egypt until the death of Herod (73 BC-4 AD), when an angel of the Lord appeared again to Joseph while he slept, telling him that it was now safe for their return to Israel.[1]

With joyful hearts Mary and Joseph then left Egypt to return to their home country, not to the territory of Judea where Archelaus reigned in the stead of Herod his father, but to Nazareth in Galilee - for on the journey, Joseph was warned in a dream not to take the Child to Judea.[2] The hitherto arduous and tiring journey was no longer a tedious affair, for the joy of the little Lord Jesus filled their hearts with an ecstasy that made the time and distance pass all too quickly. As He sat perched upon the donkey, or walked alongside in the thick sand, their precious Infant King noted everything around Him with an enthralled wonderment at God's awesome creation: the sound of the swishing sand, the dazzling sunlight, the sight of a distant carrion encircling the heavens, the cool water as it washed away the dryness from His throat - all these things were a delightful thrill to His childlike innocence; even the fine grains of sand as He gleefully trickled their softness through His tiny fingers, amazing at the infinitesimal jewelled lights glistening off the grains as they caught the sun's rays. And at night, the vast array of bright stars scattered across the universe, shone back through His large wonder-filled eyes in joyful lustre.

What rejoicing when Mary and Joseph finally reached the outskirts of Nazareth and were able to show the precious Christ Child His new home.[3] Lovingly Mary tendered to His every need, while Joseph worked quickly to make a wooden bed for

---

[1] Matt. 2:19-20
[2] Matt. 2:21-23
[3] Matt. 2:23

Jesus to lay down His sweet head. What energized love, pure joy, peace and serenity filled every corner of that blessed house as the Holy Family spent their loving days together, giving thanks to Almighty God and continuing to marvel in His great Goodness. And so the Child Jesus grew into boyhood, gaining in strength, and filled with wisdom, the grace of God being within Him.[4]

Then came an event to trouble the tranquility of those peaceful days, and bring closer to home the reality of God's plan of salvation for the world.

The Holy Family were in the habit of travelling to and from Jerusalem each year for the solemn Feast of the Pasch,[5] and the return journey on this occasion began like all the others with an early start from Jerusalem. The sun was already a full ball on the far horizon, promising the start of another scorching day. The air was filled with the echoing sounds of an early awakening in the city – the persistent deep braying of hungry mules sharply contrasting to the high-pitched shouting of the early morning vendors as they hustled and bustled their way through the crowds. Having celebrated the Pasch, families and friends were gathering themselves and their possessions to make the long journey back to their homes in the near and distant regions around the Jordan.

Mary and Joseph were already awake and gathering their few possessions. Jesus, now a young lad of twelve, had risen early too and was gone from their temporary dwelling, anxious to spend His last few hours in this fascinating city.

Typical to such journeys, Mary and Joseph separated to join up with the caravans divided into men and women, helping their parties to prepare for the long walk ahead. It took some hours to finalize preparations and organize the noisy, excited gatherings.

---

[4] Luke 2:40
[5] Luke 2:41-42

Eventually all was ready and the groups began hustling their way through the crowded city streets, aiming for the vast main gates that led the way out of Jerusalem.

Once past the thick green forests of almond, olive and pine trees that surrounded the city's outer walls in those times, the colourful columns moved slowly through the harsh wilderness of the Judean desert heading Northward, their laughter and chatter rising high into the sky - menfolk calling to each other in cheerful banter, the womenfolk chattering in groups amongst themselves, their small children running in and out of the moving masses, giggling and squealing, unable to contain the happy excitement of their newfound adventure. Only at midday did the merry band stop to seek shelter from the intense heat of the blistering sun under erected awnings, and to partake of a little food.

As the sun began dipping over the distant horizon, the segregated columns broke up to seek out their men and womenfolk and make preparations for their evening meal, prayers and various sleeping arrangements. Mary and Joseph were happy to finally find each other amidst the medley of moving masses. *"Jesus – Where is Jesus?"* were Mary's first words on perceiving that Joseph was alone. A bewildered look crossed that gentle man's features, for he had thought that Jesus was with Mary all the while. A moment of absolute silence passed between them – followed by a bewildered sense of disbelief as they stared at each other. In the next instant, they instinctively turned to search among family, friends and neighbours – their searching turning to alarm as they would return to each other at intervals, similarly empty-handed. No-one had seen Jesus.[6] He had not been with the happy, carefree band of youngsters or the older boys who would have favoured His company. As darkness settled over the myriad of flickering fire-lights, Mary fell to her knees in earnest prayer, Joseph by

---

[6] Luke 2:43-44

her side. What could have happened to their precious Son? Why was He not here with them? The voice of Simeon's bleak prophecy took hold of the gentle Virgin's heart, twisting a knife of frenzied fear into her soul.[7] Joseph put a comforting arm around the heartbroken frame, his own frantic thoughts hidden in silent anguish as he assured Mary all would be well. She must rest now and they would make the long journey back to Jerusalem at first light.[8]

The few hours left of that night passed fitfully, neither Joseph nor Mary slept peacefully. The early dawn was still a pale twilight when the two arose, their faces long and drawn. Quickly they gathered their few possessions and turned toward Jerusalem. In-between the never-ending columns of sleeping forms they tiptoed, struggling to straddle masses of shapeless bundles and avoid the burning embers of smoldering fires before the growing dawn brought the hustle and bustle of early morning risers to impede their progress. At last Mary and Joseph were alone in the desert wilderness, doggedly striding through the sand - their frantic desire to reach Jerusalem giving impetus to their stride. With every step came the disturbing anxiety over the loss of their twelve-year old Boy, fear of what had become of Him, of where He might be, of what dangers He may be facing. Stalwartly Joseph tried to console Mary, manfully hiding his own deepening fears as the day drew painfully onward.

Finally, as the early afternoon sun over-shadowed them with its searing heat, like a welcome mirage they gratefully perceived the gates of Jerusalem, piercing the distant skyline. Closer and larger the mirage mushroomed on the horizon, until finally, by day's end they had reached the shade of its mighty portals. By morning the closed gates would be opened to allow entry into the big city and at last the weary Parents fell asleep, comforted in the knowledge that their precious Jesus would soon be found.

---

[7] Luke 2:34-35
[8] Luke 2:45

As the huge gates swung open, Mary and Joseph struggled to squeeze past the exiting caravans of camels and groups of herdsmen noisily shepherding their flocks of goats, sheep and cattle through the vast entranceway, only to be met by the further early morning chaos of big city life within: vendors busily piling high their tables of various wares, crowds of hurrying, scurrying early risers vociferously adding to the general mayhem. But the heart-sore Parents were anxious only to work their way through the narrow, winding streets – stopping at the homes of local family and friends to enquire as to the whereabouts of their precious Son. As their fruitless search progressed, they recalled Jesus' fascination with the Temple, set high in the heart of Jerusalem, clearly visible from every angle of the city. Mary and Joseph anxiously set forth to reach it before nightfall. Painfully they dragged their weary feet up the long flight of wide stone steps leading up to the grand entrance of this magnificent structure they had come to know so well over the years.

Once inside the immense open corridors that made up this amazing architectural icon, the heart-sore Parents made quick progress to the place where they had but three days previously celebrated the Pasch. As their steps neared the familiar spot, Mary paused for a moment, her heart missing a beat in wondrous disbelief at the distant familiar sound of her beloved Son's voice. Yes, she could hear it clearly now, its youthful high tones rising into the vastness of the vaulted ceilings – it was truly Him, her treasured Boy. Joseph, at her side, gently ushered her forward as she trod with hesitant steps at first and then she was running, tripping over her long robe, caught before she could stumble by her Protector's strong hands. *"Jesus, Jesus!"* – the urgent strains of her excited voice echoed through the edifying chambers. Around the Boy, a group of priestly doctors were gathered in absolute admiration.[9] This beautiful Child had them enthralled in amazement as they hung on His every word.

---

[9] Luke 2:46-48

Of what manner of youngster could this be, who knew so much about the Word of God and spoke with so much wisdom? They would have continued pressing Him with eager questions, but their attention was caught by the sight of Mary and Joseph, anxiously determined to reach the object of their total wonderment. What sweet relief and pure joy as Mother and Child were reunited, Joseph promptly enjoining their warm embrace.

How the Blessed Mother had longed for this moment that for so many long drawn-out hours had eluded her. With eyes filled with tears of happiness, she gently chided the precious Boy in her arms, saying *"We have sought thee sorrowing"* - but with great tenderness, Jesus responded, *"How is it that you sought me? Did you not know that I must be about my Father's business?"*[10]

Dear Mary, Mother of Hope,
May I be inspired and guided by your holy example
to never give up but to seek and find God in this busy world
and to pray for Heavenly Wisdom.

---

[10] Luke 2:48-50

Chapter 7

Baptism of Jesus

It is not known when the Blessed Virgin's devoted guardian and protector, Joseph, passed over from this life leaving Mary a widow. We only know that after the eventful journey home from the Feast of the Pasch, Mary and Joseph returned to Nazareth with their beloved Jesus, where He remained with them in loving submission to their parental authority and guidance - all the while growing in age, wisdom and grace before God and men.[1]

What joyfulness, peace, tranquility, love and tender devotion would have abounded in that Holy Home, for in truth the very Gift of Life, God Incarnate Himself, abided therein.

It goes without saying that Mary would have followed the news of Elizabeth and Zachary's only son John, spoken of by Isaias the prophet[2] as the one to announce the coming of the Messiah, her Son Jesus – *a witness to testify to the Light, the true Light which enlightens everyone.*[3]

News spread quickly when John began preaching in the desert of Judea and all the country about the River Jordan, confirming that *"I am the one spoken of by Isaias the prophet; I am the voice of one crying in the desert".*[4]

He would call out to the crowds: *"Prepare the way of the Lord! Make straight His paths! Repent! For the Kingdom of Heaven is at hand."*[5]

---

[1] Luke 2:51-52
[2] Matt. 3:3
[3] John 1:7-9
[4] Isaias 40:30
[5] Matt. 3:1-3

The people were fascinated when they heard and saw John for his powerful voice reached out across the hills and valleys; he wore rough clothing, his garment being of camel hair, with a leather girdle about his waist, and it was rumoured he ate locusts and wild honey.

They came out from Jerusalem and all Judea, and all the surrounding countryside to hear him - and to be baptized by him in the River Jordan, anxious to confess their sins and be cleansed, and be welcomed as Children of God.

Even the Pharisees and Sadducees followed the crowds to see the cause of the commotion. When John spotted them standing afar, he pointed a finger at them and boldly proclaimed: *"Brood of vipers! Who has shown you how to flee from the wrath to come? Bear fruit worthy of repentance, and do not presume to say within yourselves, 'We have Abraham for our ancestor', for I tell you, God is able from these stones to raise up children to Abraham. Even now the axe is lying at the root of the trees; every tree therefore that does not bear good fruit, is to be cut down, and thrown into the fire."*[6]

The chief priests and scribes turned and shuffled away, muttering amongst themselves in indignation, although there were some of them who were troubled by the words and would later come back to John and be baptized.

Turning to the crowds, John told them, *"There is one, more powerful than me, who is coming; I am not worthy to stoop down and untie the thong of his sandals. I have baptized you with water but He will baptize you with the Holy Ghost and with fire. He holds a winnowing fan in His hand, and He will thoroughly clean out the threshing floor and will gather His wheat into the barn; but the chaff He will burn up with unquenchable fire."*[7] Intently the people listened to his words

---

[6] Matt. 3:7-10
[7] Matt. 3:11-12; Mark 1:1-8

and couldn't wait to see the Messiah of whom John spoke so passionately.

And so Jesus appeared one day, His tall cloaked figure striding purposefully down the steep incline toward the River Jordan.

In the dim light of that cloudy day, John rubbed his eyes in disbelief, instantly recognizing Him whom he so admired yet scarcely believing the evidence of his own eyes. He watched in amazement as Jesus drew closer, stepping into the shallow grey waters of the Jordan and splashing his way determinedly toward him.

Even greater was his wonderment when Jesus, on reaching His dumb-struck cousin, requested that John baptize Him. *"It is I who ought to be baptized by You, and yet You come to me?"*[8] John stammered.

But gently Jesus responded, *"Let it be so now, for so it becomes us to fulfill the law."*[9]

With quiet humility and deep reverence, John then proceeded to baptize the Messiah - and as Jesus rose up from the waters, so the grey clouds overhead suddenly parted and miraculously John saw the Spirit of God like a dove descending upon the Divine Son.

Even as the Baptist fell to his knees, his eyes wide with awe, he heard a voice from Heaven saying, *"This is my beloved Son, in whom I am well pleased."*[10]

What an amazing affirmation. What heart-warming news to reach the humble Virgin's ears. Yet Mary's heart was troubled

---

[8] Matt. 3:13-14
[9] Matt. 3:15
[10] Matt. 3:16-17

knowing that her Divine Son would now go forth and become known - to be loved by many, but despised too by those who would reject the Son of Man.

Dear Mary, most Holy and Saintly Virgin,
May I be inspired and guided by your holy example
to become a Child of Christ and to honour my Baptismal vows.

Chapter 8

Miracle at Cana

After the baptism of Jesus, He was led by the Spirit into the desert to be tempted by the devil.[1] The forty days and nights that followed were lonely ones for His Blessed Mother for she knew, with a fearful certainty, that her beloved Son would be doing battle with the evil one. Such a conquering He would have to achieve in order to continue His mission on earth, but Mary felt comforted that the angels of God would be ministering to her Jesus in His tired, hungry and thirsty moments.[2]

Imagine her joy when she finally heard that her Son had re-appeared; He was back in Galilee and had been seen walking with a group of followers, preaching the gospel of the Kingdom of God, saying, *"The time is now come. The Kingdom of God is at hand: Repent, and believe the good news."*[3]

How Mary longed to see her Jesus. On the third day, she hastened to the little town of Cana, just south of Nazareth, to attend a wedding feast, excited over the prospect that her Son would be there as He too was an invited guest.[4] The feast was a grand occasion. Amidst the throng of wedding guests, Mary found Jesus, His handsome face bronzed by the heat of the desert, His golden brown hair falling about His broad shoulders. He looked down at His Mother with loving tenderness, instantly understanding her concern, His eyes gently consoling her. For there was that air about the Divine Son that instantly brought a comforting peace and joy into the soul. All those around were drawn to His Presence. Mary promptly embraced her Son with great rejoicing and thanksgiving in her heart.

---

[1] Matt. 4:1
[2] Mark 1:12-13
[3] Mark 1, 14-15
[4] John 2:1-2

With Jesus were His newfound disciples. They gathered around the Blessed Mother and eagerly made themselves known to her. First, Simon the son of Jona (whom Jesus had named Simon Peter, he hastily added) with Andrew his brother; they told her they had spotted Jesus walking by the Sea of Galilee,[5] His tall cloaked frame cutting an impressive figure as He strode along the wet sand toward them. They had been amazed when He had approached just as they were about to cast their fishing nets into the water, saying to them, *"Come, follow me, and I will make you fishers of men."*[6] Both brothers had promptly left their nets and followed Him,[7] for so drawn to Jesus were they that they could not help themselves, nor did they question their own hearts. With eyes filled with an excited eagerness, Simon Peter recounted the summoning to Mary. His brother's eyes reflected the same enthusiasm as he quietly affirmed Simon Peter's sentiments, adding that when he had been with John the Baptist earlier, the Baptist had pointed out her Son to him, saying *"Behold the Lamb of God".*[8]

Then came forward, James with John his brother, the sons of Zebedee. They were known as the Sons of Thunder, they would have laughingly told her. They had been in a ship with their father, Zebedee, mending their fishing nets, and they too had been filled with wonder when Jesus had called them. Without question they had left their nets and their father, and followed Him,[9] equally filled with an inexplicable excitement. It was the same with Philip and Nathanael. Philip was of Bethsaida, he said, the same town as Andrew and Simon Peter,[10] and when Jesus had asked that he follow Him, he had hastily gone to Nathanael, and told him that he had *found Him of whom*

---

[5] Matt. 4:18
[6] Matt. 4:18
[7] Matt. 4:19
[8] John 1:36
[9] Matt. 4:21-22
[10] John 1:44

Moses in the law and the prophets did write, Jesus the son of Joseph of Nazareth![11]

Mary's heart soared at the disciples' depth of faith and words of affirmation, although her poor heart continued to be afflicted by great sadness as she realized the outcome of such a public revelation. But her beloved Son was with her now, and she would enjoy all the time she had with Him and savour every precious moment.

As the wedding feast progressed it became apparent that the wine was failing. Wine not only symbolized life but also the overflowing of Divine blessing and it was an important ingredient in any Jewish wedding ceremony, the concluding rites of which would involve seven blessings recited over the wine. Mary, filled with compassion over the plight of the bride and groom, turned to Jesus and with great faith, softly pleaded *"They have no wine"*.[12] All too well did Mary understand the importance of her request, as indeed did her Son Incarnate. He looked at her with great tenderness, determined yet to seek her full acceptance of what both Mother and Son knew so perfectly was to be. Gently and lovingly, He whispered back, *"Woman, what is that to me and to you? My hour is not yet come"*.[13] With the tenderest of understanding in the smile she returned Him, Mary beckoned to the waiters, and as they approached, indicating her Son she told them, *"Do whatever He tells you to do."*[14]

Jesus, pointing to the six water pots of stone used for the Jewish Purification ceremony, instructed the waiters to fill them with water.[15] They obeyed without hesitation, wondering at what manner of command this could be. When they had filled

---

[11] John 1:45
[12] John 2:3
[13] John 2:4
[14] John 2:5
[15] John 2:6-7

them to the brim[16] they then turned again to Jesus. *"Draw out now, and carry to the chief steward of the feast"*[17] Jesus bid them. Without question, they rushed a jar over to the chief steward for him to taste. And tasting it, the steward marveled at its goodness, and not knowing from where it came, he went quickly over to the bridegroom, and demanded to know why the best wine had been left till the end, when it was customary to serve the best wine first and only the worst after all had drank their fill![18]

This was the first of Jesus' public miracles, which caused His disciples, having witnessed the manifestation of His glory, to be over-awed, and they instantly believed in Him.[19]

Mary looked on with joy and quiet reserve. Such a manifestation of the Messiah's glory would set the events in motion that would inevitably cause her much pain and heartache. What a powerful faith she displayed in her Son's ability to perform such a miracle, and what great compassion she showed for those in need of God's help and mercy. She had interceded for the bride and groom and their guests by loving supplication to her Divine Son, a role she would continue to play not only throughout her lifetime, but throughout the history of mankind.

Dear Mary, Mother of Perpetual Succour,
May I be inspired and guided by your holy example
to trust in God's Goodness and Mercy to hear all my prayers,
begging your powerful intercession on my behalf.

---

[16] John 2:7
[17] John 2:8
[18] John 2:6-10
[19] John 2:11

Chapter 9

Proclamation of the Kingdom

After that eventful occasion of the Wedding Feast of Cana, Jesus returned to Nazareth, his hometown where He was brought up, and went into the synagogue according to His custom on the Sabbath day. When Jesus stood up to read from the book of Isaias, the prophet of old who was well known to the people, He unfolded the book and found and read from the place where it was written: *"The Spirit of the Lord is upon me and He has appointed me to preach the gospel to the poor; He has sent me to heal the contrite of heart, to preach deliverance to the captives, and sight to the blind, to set free those who are down-trodden, to preach the acceptable year of the Lord, and the day of reward."* Then He folded the book, gave it back to the high priest, and sat down. All eyes in the synagogue were fixed on Him.[1] Then Jesus spoke. *"This day this Scripture is fulfilled in your ears".*[2] Slowly the words began to sink in as all who heard pondered upon them in amazement. *"Is not this the son of Joseph?"*[3] they muttered amongst themselves, for many had known the humble carpenter while Jesus was growing up, and were wondering at these words of wisdom from the mouth of the Boy they had known.

When the whisperings had died down, Jesus then quietly addressed the assembly: *"Doubtless you will say to me this simile: Physician, heal yourself: as great things as we have heard done in Capharnaum, do also here in your own country. Yet I say to you, no prophet is accepted in his own country. In truth I say to you, there were many widows in the days of Elias in Israel, when Heaven was shut up three years and six months and there was a great famine throughout all the earth. And to none of them was Elias sent, but to Sarepta of Sidon, to a widow*

---

[1] Luke 4:16-20
[2] Luke 4:21
[3] Luke 4:22

47

woman. And there were many lepers in Israel in the time of Eliseus the prophet: and none of them was cleansed but Naaman the Syrian."[4] Silence momentarily reigned in the synagogue as the townspeople inwardly battled over the words. Widows? Syrians? Why would mere widows and Syrians of all people receive such favours? For such was the thinking of those times.

Gradually the silence broke down as the high priests and townsfolk began to mutter amongst themselves. Indignation and anger followed their initial bewilderment, building up to a vexatious crescendo. With one accord, they rose up and shoved at Jesus, pushing Him out of the synagogue and through the narrow city streets to the brow of the hill upon which Nazareth was built, determined to cast Him down headlong. Imagine their amazement when Jesus miraculously passed through their midst and went on His way![5] For it was not yet time for the Son of Man to be delivered into the hands of His enemies.

Mary was deeply distressed when she heard how her hometown had rejected her beloved Son. But Jesus consoled her and together with His disciples and all those who remained faithful to Him, left Nazareth with His Mother and went to Capharnaum on the sea coast, along the borders of Zabulon and Nephthalim, which town then became their new home base in fulfillment of the prophecy of Isaias the prophet: *Land of Zabulon and land of Nephthalim, the way of the sea beyond the Jordan, Galilee of the Gentiles: The people who sit in darkness have seen a great Light.*[6] Unlike Nazareth, a mountainous and isolated hamlet, Capharnaum was a crossroad of primary importance, being along the Damascus highway. It was also a town set apart from the big centres like Tiberias, where Herod Antipas had set up his capital. Thus Jesus was able to spread His message to many without running too soon into trouble with the political and religious leaders of the times. Even the relations

---

[4] Luke 4:23-27
[5] Luke 4:28-30
[6] Matt. 4:13-16

between the inhabitants of Capharnaum and the Romans were, at the time, surprisingly cordial. It was a Roman centurion who built the synagogue for the Jewish community there, while the elders of Capharnaum reciprocated in kindness and were later seen to plead with Jesus, begging Him to heal the centurion's servant.[7] Also in contrast to Nazareth, the population of Capharnaum was highly diversified, being fishermen, farmers, artisans, merchants, publicans - hard working inhabitants, parsimonious, and more open-minded to Christ's message of salvation. Indeed the town was home to a number of the disciples, like the fishermen James and John, and Matthew the publican.

So it was with some relief that Mary found her home with Jesus in Capharnaum. On the Sabbath, her Divine Son, being in the power of the Holy Spirit, [8] taught in the town's synagogue, and all who heard Him were astonished at His doctrine, for He would teach them as one having authority, and not as the local scribes.[9] One such occasion, there appeared in the synagogue a man with an unclean spirit, crying out, *What have we to do with you, Jesus of Nazareth? Are you come to destroy us? I know who you are, the Holy One of God!*[10] To the amazement of those standing around, who were both alarmed by the angry words of the demented soul and perplexed over their pronouncement, Jesus commanded, *Speak no more, and come out of the man,* and instantly the unclean spirit departed.[11] *What thing is this?* they questioned amongst themselves, *What is this new doctrine? For with power He commands even*

---

[7] Luke 7:1-10, Matt. 8:5-13
[8] Luke 4:14; Mark 1:39; Act of Apostles 10:38
[9] Mark 1:21-22
[10] Mark 1:24
[11] Mark 1:25

the unclean spirits, and they obey Him."[12] And rapidly the fame of Jesus spread throughout all the country of Galilee.[13]

And in the same way that Capharnaum became known as the hometown of Jesus and Mary, so did the disciple Simon Peter's home become known as the house of Jesus[14] and Mary.[15] The same day as the healing of the man with the unclean spirit, after leaving the synagogue to return home, Simon Peter's mother-in-law was found in bed with a high fever at the house. At once Jesus went to her side. Gently He took her hand - and immediately the fever left her so that she found herself joyfully able to help serve at the table.[16] Quickly news of the miraculous healing spread throughout the town and that evening, as the sun dipped below the horizon, there appeared at the house gates a large crowd of townspeople, bringing with them all who were sick, beseeching Jesus to help them. In His infinite mercy and compassion, He healed many all through that night, not only those troubled by illness or disease, but also those possessed by demons.[17]

The following morning, Mary found Jesus had risen very early and left the house, seeking the solitude of the surrounding desert so that He might pray to His Father in Heaven.[18] She smiled to herself in loving understanding and went to kneel herself in prayer in the quiet solitude of her small room; how well she recognized the need for her Son to communicate with

---

[12] Mark 1:27
[13] Mark 1:28
[14] Mark 1:29-34; Matt. 8:14; Luke 4:38
[15] Many years later, after the destruction of Capharnaum, archaeological discoveries were able to confirm that Peter's house was a very large one, consisting of several roofed rooms clustered around a spacious courtyard and big enough to house all of Peter's families, together with Jesus and Mary.
[16] Mark 1:29-31; Matt. 8:14-17; Luke 4:38-39
[17] Mark 1:32-34; Matt. 8:14-17; Luke 4:38-39
[18] Mark 1:35

the Eternal Father, knowing as she did, His nature to be both human and Divine.

As the morning broke through its golden sunrise, Simon Peter and the disciples went looking for Jesus, finding Him on His knees in the fine sand, deep in prayer. Softly Peter approached and interrupted, saying that the people were again looking for Him. Stiffly their Master rose, smiling at their eagerness. Gently He responded, *"Let us go into the neighbouring towns and cities, that I may preach there also; for to this purpose am I come".*[19]

Jesus then went throughout Galilee, preaching in the synagogues, casting out devils and healing the sick;[20] and all the people wondered at His glory.[21]

And there came to Him one day, a leper – his gnarled and sore-ridden body a terrible sight to behold. Everyone who saw him, leapt back in fear, for lepers were not allowed into the towns but were banished to a remote area so that their disease could not contaminate others. He knelt before Jesus and implored, *"If you choose, you can make me clean".*[22] The Divine Son looked down at him with great compassion, and stretching forth His hand, He touched the leper. All who witnessed the touching were instantly reviled and a gasp of horror rose up from the onlookers. But Jesus, with great tenderness, told the leper, *"I do choose. Be made clean!"*[23] and immediately the leprosy departed from the man and he was made whole again. The crowds were astounded and now a cry of wonderment rose from their lips. Sending the cleansed leper on his way, the Son of Man charged him, *"See you tell no one; but go, show yourself to the high priest, and offer for your cleansing the things that*

---

[19] Mark 1:37-38
[20] Mark 1:39
[21] Luke 4:14-15
[22] Mark 1:40
[23] Mark 1:41

Moses commanded, as a testimony to them".[24] The man, however, beside himself with joy, pranced through the crowds, pulling off his outer garments to show them his healed face, hands and arms, for he could not contain his excitement; without thought to his Saviour's words, he advertised his healing to all and everyone, so that people poured into the city in search of the Healer, so much so that Jesus could no longer go about freely, for the crowds flocked to Him from all sides.[25]

And so Mary's Divine Son continued His travels throughout all Galilee, teaching in the synagogues, preaching the gospel of the Kingdom, and healing all manner of sickness among the people. His fame spread even into neighbouring Syria, so that the crowds flocked to Him from near and far, from all over Galilee, from Decapolis, Jerusalem, Judea, and even from beyond the Jordan,[26] bringing with them their sick with various diseases, the deaf and dumb, the lame, lunatics, those with palsy and those tormented by devils; and the compassionate Messiah cured them all. And Mary rejoiced in the knowledge of her Son's great love for the people, His teachings and wondrous miracles. She would spend every opportunity she could, following Him around the countryside with Mary of Cleophas (her sister-in-law, and mother of James and Jude, Simon and Joseph),[27] Joanna (wife of Chusa, Herod's steward), Salome (mother of John and James, the sons of Zebedee), Mary Magdalen (whom Jesus had healed of seven devils), one named Susanna, and others who were equally anxious to care for our beloved Saviour.[28]

Of the disciples there were twelve whom her Son had named as His Apostles: Simon (whom He surnamed Peter) and Andrew his brother, James and John (Sons of Thunder), Philip and Bartholomew, Matthew and Thomas, James and Jude (sons

---

[24] Mark 1:42-44
[25] Mark 1:45
[26] Matt. 4:23-25
[27] Matt.13:55
[28] Luke 8:1-3

52

of Cleophas), Simon (who was called Zelotes), and Judas Iscariot.[29] To each of His Apostles, Jesus later gave power to preach[30] and power over unclean spirits to cast out devils, and to heal all manner of diseases and infirmities,[31] His Blessed Mother rejoicing in the expansion of her Divine Son's Kingdom on earth.

Simon Peter was the first to proclaim Jesus as *Christ, the Son of the living God.* And the Son Incarnate, recognizing that such a revelation to Peter had been revealed by His Father in Heaven, told him, *"You are Peter; and upon this rock I will build my Church, and the gates of hell will not prevail against it,"*[32] thereby appointing Simon Peter as the head of His Church on earth. *"And I will give you the keys of the Kingdom of Heaven"*[33] continued Jesus, further assigning to Peter certain powers in that key role; and *"whatever you bind on earth, shall be bound also in Heaven; and whatever you loose on earth, it shall be loosed also in Heaven,"*[34] thus giving Peter the power to cleanse away the sins of those who confessed them and wished to be saved; which latter gift Jesus later also gave to each of His other Apostles.[35]

Great too was Mary's joy when she witnessed her Son blessing the multitudes with the comforting gift of His Beatitudes – qualities to which we should all aspire in our quest to reach the eternal Kingdom:

> *Blessed are the poor in spirit: for theirs is the Kingdom of Heaven.*
> *Blessed are the meek: for they shall inherit the earth.*
> *Blessed are they who mourn: for they shall be comforted.*

---

[29] Luke 6,12-16
[30] Mark 3:14
[31] Matt. 10:1
[32] Matt. 16:16-18
[33] Matt. 16:19
[34] Matt. 16:19
[35] Matt. 18:18

Blessed are they who hunger and thirst for justice: for they shall be filled.
Blessed are the merciful: for they shall receive mercy.
Blessed are the pure of heart: for they shall see God.
Blessed are the peacemakers: for they shall be called children of God.
Blessed are they who are persecuted for justice sake: for theirs is the Kingdom of Heaven. [36]

In the early morning sunshine of that bright day, seated all around the surrounding low hills and in the valley below, the people listened with keen attentiveness to their Master, standing tall and impressive in the shade of the vale, His strong voice reaching out to all of them, inspiring their hearts with His gentle way. *"Blessed are you when people revile and persecute you, and speak all kinds of evil against you falsely on my account,"* [37] He continued. *"Rejoice and be glad, for your reward is great in Heaven – for in the same way they persecuted the prophets who were before you"*. [38] These teachings of her beloved Son were a source of great comfort to the Blessed Virgin over the many days and years to follow - as indeed they should be to us all, who have faith in the Word of God.

There was so much that Jesus taught, valuable lessons for the guidance of all who long to make their home with the Eternal God in Heaven. *"You will love the Lord your God with your whole heart, and with your whole soul, and with your whole mind,"* [39] Jesus gently commanded, adding: *"This is the greatest and the first commandment. And the second is like it: You will love one another as I have loved you."* [40]

And Jesus warned them sternly: *"Woe to you who are rich: for you have your consolation. Woe to you who are filled: for*

---

[36] Matt. 5:3-10
[37] Matt.5:11
[38] Matt. 5:12
[39] Matt. 22:37
[40] Matt. 22:38-39

you shall hunger. Woe to you who now laugh: for you shall mourn and weep. Woe to you when men bless you for so did your fathers to the false prophets,"[41] but with great gentleness He further commanded, "Love your enemies; do good, and lend, hoping for nothing in return: and your reward shall be great, and you will be called children of the Highest; be merciful, as your Father also is merciful; judge not, and you will not be judged; condemn not, and you will not be condemned; forgive, and you will be forgiven; give, and it will be given to you."[42] The people were silent, eagerly absorbing all that Jesus taught them.

And He taught them how to pray to His Father in Heaven, saying: "Thus therefore will you pray: Our Father who art in Heaven, hallowed be Thy name. Thy Kingdom come. Thy Will be done on earth as it is in Heaven. Give us this day our daily Bread. And forgive us our trespasses as we forgive those who trespass against us. And lead us not into temptation but deliver us from evil. Amen." and He added, "For if you forgive those who have offended you, so your heavenly Father will forgive you your offences. But if you do not forgive, neither will your Father forgive you."[43]

He spoke with such authority yet a firm tenderness, His voice carrying far across the hills, valleys and plains to the vast crowds of people who would continue to gather in their droves, eager to listen to and heed the voice of the Messiah.

Watching her Son and listening to Him were precious moments to Mary who cherished all that He said and did, keeping everything close to her heart and giving thanks to Almighty God. She was also present or heard about all manner of wondrous deeds wherein her Divine Son manifested His glory: how He fed the five thousand on five loaves and two

---

[41] Luke 6:21-26
[42] Luke 6:35-38
[43] Matt. 6:9-15

fish,[44] and four thousand with seven loaves and a few fish;[45] how He walked upon the waters,[46] and calmed the seas;[47] drove away demented spirits;[48] made whole the blind,[49] the dumb[50] and the lame;[51] cured lepers;[52] healed Roman,[53] Gentile,[54] and Jew alike; indeed how the people were healed of their various sicknesses;[55] some simply by touching His garment,[56] wherever they had great faith;[57] how He raised back to life the son of a widow woman in the city of Naim[58] and the daughter of Jairus[59] - so great was the Son of Man's love for the people, His deep compassion and infinite mercy.

One important such event occurred in the lives of Lazarus, Martha and Mary (believed to be Mary Magdalen[60]), a family very dear to Jesus and His gentle Mother. They lived in Bethany, a village on the East slope of Mt. Olivet, a short distance from Jerusalem. On this occasion (just days before Palm Sunday), Lazarus had fallen very sick. So his sisters sent word to Jesus, with the message *"Lord, he whom you love is ill."* Gently, Jesus responded, *"This illness does not lead to death, rather it is for the glory of God so that the Son of God may be glorified through it"* and, understanding not His words, those who heard were amazed that, in spite of the great love He had

---

[44] Mark 6:41-44; Matt. 14:16-21
[45] Matt. 15:34-38
[46] Mark 6:48-50; Matt. 14:25-32
[47] Mark 6:51; Matt. 8:24-26
[48] Luke 8:27-33
[49] Luke 18:35-43
[50] Luke 11:14
[51] Matt. 9:2-7
[52] Luke 17:11-19
[53] Luke 7:2-10
[54] Mark 7:25-30
[55] Luke 13:11-13; 14:2-4
[56] Luke 8:43-44; Matt. 14:36
[57] Mark 2:3-5; John 4:46-50
[58] Luke 7:12-15
[59] Luke 8:41-42, 49-55; Matt. 9, 1:38
[60] John 11:2; Catholic Encyclopedia: St. Mary Magdalen

for the family, Jesus did not go at once to Lazarus but remained where He was for two whole days. He then said to His disciples, *"Let us go now into Judea. Lazarus our friend sleeps; but I go that I may awake him."* And they replied, *"Lord, if he has fallen asleep, he will be alright."* But Jesus, knowing all things, was speaking of his death and not the repose of sleep, and gently but firmly He told them so, adding, *"and I am glad for your sakes that I was not there, so that you may believe: but let us go to him."*[61] Those who heard were mystified.

When they finally arrived at Bethany it was to discover that Lazarus had been dead four days already and had been buried in a tomb. And there was great sadness for Lazarus had been much loved; their home was filled with friends and neighbours anxious to comfort the weeping sisters. As soon as Martha heard that Jesus was coming, she rushed out to meet Him on the way, leaving her sister Mary at home. She flung herself at her Master's feet, beseeching Him, *"Lord, if you had been here, my brother would not have died. But I know that whatever you ask of God, God will give to you."* Jesus tenderly took her hands and looking into her pleading eyes, assured her, *"Your brother will rise again."* But Martha remained insistent as she returned, *"I know that he will rise again, in the resurrection at the last day".* Jesus then smiled down at her, *"I am the Resurrection and the Life: he who believes in Me, although he be dead, will live: anyone who lives and believes in Me, will not die for ever. Do you believe this?"* and she murmured through her tears, *"Yes, Lord, I believe that you are the Messiah, the Son of God, the One who has come into this world."* Then, joyfully Martha ran back to the house to fetch Mary that she might hear our Saviour's words too. Secretly from the mourners around her, she whispered, *"The Master is on His way, and calls for you".* Her sister rose from her seat of mourning and the two hurried toward where Martha had seen Jesus at the outskirts of the village. The townspeople followed, not understanding where the sisters were

---

[61] John 11:1-15

going, except perhaps to their brother's graveside to weep. When Mary saw Jesus, she too fell at His feet, sobbing, *"Lord, if you had been here, my brother would not have died"*. Jesus felt great compassion for the weeping sister at His feet, and seeing the crowd of people who had followed, He then asked where they had laid Lazarus. *"Lord, come and see,"*[62] they said.

Quickly they crossed the ground to the place where Lazarus had been buried, in a cave the entrance of which had been covered with a great stone. Jesus, His eyes filled with tears, could hear some of the townspeople mumbling *"See how He loved him"* and others muttering *"Could not He who opened the eyes of the man born blind, have kept this man from dying?"* The Messiah stood, tall and silent, on the high rocky ground, looking down at the mournful sight of the sepulcher. Then He ordered those around Him, *"Take away the stone"*. Martha objected for a moment, concerned that her brother had been dead four days and his body already decaying. But Jesus said to her, *"Did I not tell you that if you believe you will see the glory of God?"* So they rolled away the stone, and the Son of God, looking up to Heaven, cried out, *"Father, I thank You for having heard me. And I know that You always hear me but I am saying this for the sake of the people standing here, so that they may believe that it is You who sent me."* Then looking down at the grave, He called out, *"Lazarus, come out"*. All around were silent, staring at the open entrance of the cave. Then a cry of awe went up from the crowd, for there appeared at the opening, a tall figure, bound completely in bandages from head to foot and with a cloth binding his head. He stood there, swaying a little in the bright sunlight. And immediately at Jesus' command to loose him, they rushed to unwind the bands, rejoicing and amazing that he who was dead was now alive.[63]

Such is the immeasurable love the Divine Son has for His people. His Blessed Mother's great faith in the ability and desire

---

[62] John 11:16-34
[63] John 11:35-45

of her loving Son to comfort and heal would strengthen her in times when she faced hardship and heartache[64] - as it should be so for the Reader too.

One such occasion was the sad news of the terrible death of her beloved John the Baptist at the hands of Herod the Tetrarch. Herod feared the Baptist, whom he believed to be raised from the dead, and was distressed when John told him it was not lawful for Herod to have Herodias, his brother's wife. So to keep John quiet, he had the Baptist arrested and thrown into prison. He did not want to put John to death, fearing reprisal from the people who looked upon the Baptist as a prophet.[65] However, on Herod's birthday, it was said that the daughter of Herodias danced before the court, pleasing the Tetrarch so much that he promised with an oath to give the girl whatever she would ask of him. The daughter promptly turned to her mother Herodias – and, under her mother's instruction, went back to Herod, saying *Give me the head of John the Baptist.* Indeed the Tetrarch was struck sad at the request for although he feared him, he liked and respected the Baptist. Yet because of his oath, and to please them who sat with him at table, he commanded that it be done; he had John beheaded there and then, and the head was placed in a dish and presented before Herod, who, unable to look upon his shameful act, immediately beckoned that it be given to the waiting damsel – who took the gruesome dish and gave it to her mother.[66]

When the Apostles heard what had happened, they took the body of John the Baptist and buried it, and then went to break the news to their Master.[67]

Acutely saddened, Jesus withdrew in a boat by Himself to a deserted place set apart from the multitudes,[68] and in His

---

[64] Ps.129
[65] Matt. 14:1-5
[66] Matt. 14:6-11
[67] Matt. 14:12
[68] Matt.14:13

humanity prayed to His Father in Heaven. Mary received the news with equal devastation, and on her knees in the quiet of her small room, she similarly sought the comfort of God, the Almighty Father.

Dear Mother, Faithful servant of God,
May I be inspired and guided by your holy example
to pray for God's Comfort and Guidance
throughout my daily life.

Chapter 10
Death and Resurrection Foretold

It was in the quiet of one late afternoon, as the shadows lengthened and the sun slowly dipped below the horizon that the Son of Man gently broke the news to His Blessed Mother that the time was fast approaching when He would be betrayed into the hands of His enemies and suffer a terrible death for the salvation of men's souls. Tenderly Jesus took Mary into His arms and wiped away the large tears as they spilled down her lovely face in silent anguish, comforting her that He would rise again on the third day when she would see Him in His glory. Both Mother and Son had known that the dreaded hour would come some day; that the Scriptures would be fulfilled, for it was for this purpose that the Incarnate Son of God had come into this world.

As fear and rumour travelled easily throughout Judea, it had already come to the gentle Virgin's ears that the Pharisees (scribes) and Sadducees (chief priests) were anxious to do away with her Son. They had learned of the raising of Lazarus from the dead from a few who had witnessed the miracle and reported back to their Council; they were alarmed over the growing following of Jesus, saying amongst themselves, *"If we let him alone, all will believe in Him; and the Romans will come, and take away our place and nation"*. She had heard that they had issued an order that if anyone knew where Jesus was, he should report to the chief priests and scribes that they might arrest Him.[1] Already her beloved Jesus could no longer walk openly among the Jewish people, but had retired to Ephrem, a city in a region near the desert, where He remained with His disciples until His time was at hand.

Mary had also been aware of the growing jealousy among the Pharisees and Sadducees for some time previously, indeed

---

[1] John 11:56

since the first Feast of the Pasch after her Son's baptism by John the Baptist in the River Jordan, when Jesus had gone into the Temple at Jerusalem and become angry over something He had witnessed there. She had heard how He had beheld within the majestic arena of the Temple that day, a great busyness of oxen and sheep and doves being sold amidst much noise and furore as deals were made and money changed hands. He had stood in stony silence, taking in the shameful sight before Him. Then, making a scourge of little cords, He had driven the sheep and oxen out of the Temple, scattering them down the vast stone steps; He poured out the money of the changers and overthrew their tables. And to those selling doves, He had said: *"Take these things out of here, and make not the House of my Father a house of traffic."*[2] His disciples who were with Him had watched their Master in amazement, remembering that it was written in the Scriptures: *The zeal of thy house has eaten me up.* But those who were in the Temple had demanded to know of Jesus, *"What sign can you show us for doing this?"* to which Jesus had responded, *"Destroy this Temple, and in three days I will raise it up."* A cry of horror had gone up from the people and they had sniggered, *"Six and forty years was this Temple in the making, and you will raise it up in three days?"*[3] And so already were the seeds of discontent sown among those who would seek the death of the Son of Man.

But unbeknown to their ignorant ears, Jesus had been speaking of the temple of His Body (and indeed, much later when the Messiah was risen from the dead, His Apostles were to remember these, His words);[4] and even then, although there were many who believed in Him that day in the Temple, Jesus, knowing all things, did not entrust Himself to them, for He knew and understood what was in their hearts.[5]

---

[2] John 2:13-16
[3] John 2:17-21
[4] John 2:21-22
[5] John 2:23-25

Since that occasion in the Temple, it seemed that the Pharisees and Sadducees sought every occasion to trip up the Son of Man in an effort to discredit Him. There came a Sabbath day, after Jesus had been teaching in the synagogue, that a man approached Him whose right hand was withered. The chief priests and scribes were watching to see if Jesus would heal on the Sabbath, that they might find an accusation against Him. But Jesus knew their thoughts. He gently commanded the man, *"Stand up and come over here"*,[6] and then turning to those who would trick Him, Jesus said, *"I ask you, is it lawful on the Sabbath to do good, or to do evil; to save life, or to destroy it?"*[7] No one dared answer. Slowly Jesus looked around at each one of them, but still no one replied. Looking to the man with the withered hand, Jesus then commanded him, *"Stretch forth your hand"*, and when the man stretched forth his hand, it was instantly healed. What wondrous rejoicing for the man, but the scribes and the high priests turned away, filled with anger. They talked amongst each other what they might do to Jesus.[8] His Blessed Mother, when she heard what had transpired, had felt a continuing fear and sadness at the growing hostility among the Pharisees and Sadducees toward her Son.

Her sense of foreboding had been intensified over an incident that occurred six days before the upcoming Pasch. Jesus and His Apostles had returned to Galilee to join Lazarus for supper, and while Martha served at the table, her sister Mary took a pound of expensive ointment and proceeded to anoint the feet of Jesus, wiping His feet with her hair. Judas Iscariot, one of the Apostles, seemed disturbed by her act of kindness, grumbling that the ointment could have been sold and the money given to the poor. Jesus had replied, *"Let her alone: why do you trouble her? She has performed a good service to me. For you always have the poor with you, and you can show kindness to them whenever you wish; but you will not always*

---

[6] Luke 6:6-8
[7] Luke 6:9
[8] Luke 6:10-11

have me. *She has done what she could; she has anointed my body beforehand ready for its burial.*"[9] The gentle Mother had pondered over these words, knowing then in her heart that the time of her Divine Son's deliverance was surely close at hand.

Jesus had been preparing His Apostles too, explaining that He must go to Jerusalem, where He would suffer many things at the hands of the chief priests and scribes, and there be put to death – gently adding that on the third day He would rise again.[10] A hushed silence fell over them as they grappled with the grimness of their Master's words, each of them confused and bewildered. Peter, the first to speak, begged that this be not done to His Master, but Jesus gently rebuked him, saying, *"Get behind me, Satan"*. Then firmly He told them: *"If any man comes after me, let him deny himself, and take up his cross, and follow me. For he who saves his life, will lose it: and he who loses his life for my sake, will find it. For what does it profit a man if he gain the whole world, and suffer the loss of his own soul? Or what exchange shall a man give for his soul?"* Then smiling tenderly at their forlorn expressions, He added, *"For the Son of Man will come in the glory of His Father with His angels: and then will He render to every man according to His works."*[11] Yet still the words brought little comfort to the Apostles, for they did not fully comprehend.

To better prepare His Apostles and help them to understand, six days after the above discourse, Jesus secretly took Simon Peter and the brothers James and John up a high mountain, apart from the others. And while they were standing on the mountain top, He became transfigured before them, His face shining as the sun, His garments as white as snow. And even as the three stood entranced in wide-eyed awe, there suddenly appeared Moses and Elijah, talking with the Divine Son. Simon Peter, finding his voice, said to Jesus, *"Lord, it is good for us to be here: let us*

---

[9] John 12:1-8; Matt. 26:12; Mark 14:8
[10] Matt.16:21; Mark 8:31; Luke 9:22
[11] Matt. 16:21-27

make three tents, one for you, one for Moses, and one for Elijah" (for by revelation the Apostles' eyes were opened to recognize the ancients). But even as he spoke a bright cloud overshadowed the three figures and from out of the cloud they heard a voice saying, *"This is my beloved Son, in whom I am well pleased: Listen to Him."* The Apostles instantly fell to their knees, their faces against the earth they were so afraid. But Jesus gently touched them, saying *"Get up and do not be afraid"*, and when they looked up they saw no one else but Jesus. As they came down the mountain, the Apostles speechless with wonder, Jesus ordered them not to tell of the vision to any one till *He had risen from the dead* – words they still could not fully comprehend in spite of what they had just witnessed.[12]

Later, they asked Jesus, *"Why do the scribes say that Elijah must come first?"* and Jesus solemnly answered, *"Elijah indeed was to come and restore all things. But I say to you, that Elijah has already come, and they knew him not, but did to him whatever they had a mind."* It then dawned on the Apostles that Jesus was speaking of John the Baptist. And the Messiah added quietly, *"So also the Son of Man will suffer from them."*[13]

The people too, heard Jesus speaking of His impending death and resurrection. They were troubled by His grievous words, sensing the great depth of sadness in their Master's voice. Solemnly He told them, *"Now my soul is troubled, and what shall I say - Father, save me from this hour? No, it is for this reason that I have come to this hour."* On this occasion, as they pressed closer, they perceived the Son of Man looking upward as He softly uttered the words, *"Father, glorify thy name,"* at which point came a voice from the clouds, saying, *"I have both glorified it, and will glorify it again."* The crowd looked around at one another, speechless - some determining it was a freak rumble of thunder while others looked alarmed, believing that an angel had truly spoken to their Master. But

---

[12] Matt. 17:1-9
[13] Matt. 17:10-13

Jesus, responding to their mixed reactions, gently told them: *"This voice has come for your sake - not for mine. Now is the judgment of the world: now the Ruler of this world will be cast out. And when the Son of Man is lifted up from the earth, He will draw all people to Himself."*[14] In silence, the people struggled to understand and accept the words. Then someone from the crowd called out, *"We have heard from the law, that Christ lives for ever; so how can you say that the Son of Man must be lifted up? Who is this Son of Man?"* Tenderly, Jesus responded, *"For just a little while longer, the Light is among you. Walk while you have the Light in case the darkness overtake you. He who walks in darkness cannot see where he goes. While you have the Light, believe in the Light, that you may become children of the Light."*[15]

But still they understood not His words for their eyes were blinded and their hearts hardened.[16] And our Lord Jesus Christ, all-compassionate, all-loving Saviour, wept inwardly; as did His Blessed Mother, Mary.

Dear Mary, Mother of Unwavering Faith,
May I be inspired and guided by your holy example
to have complete Trust in God in times of trouble and fear.

---

[14] John 12:24-32
[15] John 12:34-36
[16] John 12:40

Chapter 11
Institution of the Eucharist

"*L*et not your heart be troubled" Jesus comforted His beloved Mother and Apostles. "*You believe in God, believe also in me. In my Father's house there are many mansions. If this were not so, I would not be telling you this. I go to prepare a place for you. And if I go and prepare a place for you, I will come again, and will take you to myself; so that where I am, you also may be. And to where I go, you already know, and the way you know.*"[1]

What sweet words of consolation from their Master. Being close to Jesus as His Mother was, Mary understood these words of comfort and kept them close to her heart; not only throughout the terrible hours of her beloved Son's impending suffering and death, but also throughout the long months and years ahead when she would long for Jesus to come and take her Home to Heaven to be with Him for eternity.

But His Apostles were perplexed. Thomas asked of Jesus, "*Lord, we know not to where you are going; and how can we know the way?*" Gently but firmly, Jesus confirmed His Divinity, "*I am the Way, and the Truth, and the Life. No man can come to the Father except through me. If you know me, you also know my Father: and from henceforth you will know Him, for you have seen Him.*"[2]

On a previous occasion in the synagogue in Capharnaum, Jesus had addressed the large crowd gathered there to hear His voice, "*Truly I tell you: he who believes in me, has everlasting Life. I am the Bread of Life.*"[3] The crowd had looked around at one another, wondering what the words could mean. The Divine Son, knowing what was in their hearts, continued: "*Your fathers*

---

[1] John 14:1-5
[2] John 14:5-7
[3] John 6:47-48

ate manna in the desert, and are dead. This is the Bread that comes down from Heaven so that one may eat of it and not die. I am the living Bread that came down from Heaven. Whoever eats of this Bread will live for ever; and the Bread that I will give for the life of the world is my Flesh."[4]

With much alarm, they had muttered amongst themselves, *"How can this man give us his flesh to eat?"* With tender compassion, Jesus gently but firmly reiterated, *"Very truly I tell you, unless you eat the Flesh of the Son of Man and drink His Blood, you have no Life in you. Those who eat my Flesh and drink my Blood have eternal Life and I will raise them up on the last day. For my Flesh is true food and my Blood is true drink."* Addressing their continued perplexed and troubled expressions, the Son Incarnate further stressed His words: *"Those who eat my Flesh and drink my Blood abide in me and I in them. Just as the living Father sent me, and I live because of the Father, so whoever eats me will live because of me. This is the Bread that came down from Heaven, not like that which your ancestors ate and are dead. But whoever eats this Bread will live for ever."*[5]

Jesus was speaking of His Glorified Body, not His carnal earthly body: *"Labour not for the meat which perishes, but for that which endures into Life everlasting, which the Son of Man will give you."*[6] But even the most devoted of His followers found the words difficult to understand and accept.

"Does this offend you?" their Master turned to ask them. *"What if you were to see the Son of Man ascending to where He was before? It is the spirit that gives life; the flesh is useless. The words that I have spoken to you are Spirit and Life"* and He added sorrowfully, *"Yet there are still those among you who do not believe".* Indeed, many of them could not or would not grasp the meaning of their Master's words and would walk with Him

---

[4] John 6:49-52
[5] John 6:53-59
[6] John 6:27

no more. Mary suffered a great sadness that her Son's words had fallen on so many deaf ears.

Turning to His twelve Apostles, Jesus asked them, *"Do you also wish to go away?"* It was Simon Peter who responded: *"Lord, to whom can we go? You have the words of eternal life. We have come to believe and know that You are the Christ, the Son of God."*[7] Heartwarming words to the Divine Son, although it was known to Him that *no man can come to me, unless it be given him by my Father.*[8] His gentle Mother, standing quietly close by, had smiled at Peter's quick response, her heart warmed by the Apostle's solid affirmation.

It was now approaching the Feast of the Pasch, a time that had often marked an eventful occasion in the lives of Jesus and Mary. A great multitude, having heard of the raising of Lazarus from the dead just days previously, poured into Jerusalem knowing that Jesus would be there for the Pasch; and as the Noon hour was approaching, indeed the Messiah and His Apostles were already heading toward the city.

Near the outskirts, in a little town called Bethphage, close to Mount Olivet, Jesus sent two of His Apostles to a neighbouring village to collect an ass with her colt, tethered to a tree; they were to loose the beasts and bring them to Jesus, saying, if any man should challenge them, that their Master needed the animals and would have them returned shortly.[9] When the ass and the colt were brought to Jesus, His disciples, sensing the importance of the occasion, saddled their own homespun mantles over the backs of the beasts before their King took His seat, first on the ass and then, as they reached the gates of Jerusalem, on the colt.[10]

---

[7] John 6:68-70
[8] John 6:66
[9] Matt. 21:1-3
[10] Matt 21:7

As they arrived through the city gates, they were greeted by the large crowd, many of them throwing down their cloaks before the colt; they had come out to welcome our sweet Saviour in the early afternoon sun, holding up branches of palm and olive trees in joyous greeting, crying *"Hosanna to the Son of David! Blessed is He who comes in the name of the Lord, the King of Israel!"* Joyfully they surrounded Him as He sat upon the small beast, just as it was written in the Scriptures, *Tell the daughters of Zion: Look, your King comes, humble and mounted on an ass, and then a colt, the foal of a donkey that is used to the yoke.*[11] With great love and compassion, Jesus looked around at the tumultuous gathering of happy, smiling faces, touched by their greeting; yet, knowing all things, His heart heavy at what He knew to be ahead of Him.

His Blessed Mother, too, when she heard of the joyous welcoming, shared in her Son's bitter-sweetness. Inevitably, she understood the significance of His riding the ass and then the colt – the humble ass signifying the virtues of her Son's Humility in taking on flesh in human form, His Patience in bearing all things without anger, resentment or complaint, and His Submissiveness to the Will of the Father - so great was His love for mankind; the unused colt signifying the fresh yoke that she knew Christ was to lay on those who would willingly take up the challenges that becoming a devoted follower of her Son would inevitably invoke.

Once beyond the vast portals of Jerusalem, Jesus sent Simon Peter and John into the city's centre to prepare for their Pasch, where they met a man carrying a pitcher of water and going into a large house just as Jesus had told them. The man showed them into a furnished dining room where they could prepare for the meal, and when the hour was come, Jesus took His seat at the table, along with His Twelve.

---

[11] John 12:12-15; Matt. 21:4-5

Expectantly, all eyes were turned toward their beloved Master. With a quiet gravity in His voice, they heard His alarming words that this would be the last meal He would share with them until it was *fulfilled in the Kingdom of God.*[12] The Apostles could feel His deep sadness and indeed were themselves greatly troubled. While they somberly ate, Jesus spoke to them at length, compounding His earlier teachings of God's plan of salvation for the whole world.[13]

And in confirmation of His earlier instruction, *unless you eat the Flesh of the Son of Man and drink His blood you will not have Life in you,*[14] the Divine Son then proceeded to establish the Heavenly sacrament to which He had been referring - which later became known as the Institution of the Holy Eucharist: Taking bread in His sacred hands, Jesus blessed it, broke it, and gave it to each of the Apostles, saying: *"Take this and eat it. This is my Body."* And taking the chalice filled with wine, He gave thanks to Almighty God, and handed it to them, saying: *"Take this and drink from it, all of you. For this is my Blood; the Blood of the new covenant, which will be shed for many so that sins may be forgiven. And I tell you, I will never again drink of this fruit of the vine until that day when I shall drink it with you, new, in the Kingdom of my Father."*[15]

A deathly hush fell over the Twelve as they somberly partook of the consecrated bread and wine, now miraculously transformed into Christ's Precious Body and Blood; for over the many months with our loving Saviour, they had readily seen and experienced that whenever He issued a statement or command, so His words instantly became reality and action.

Jesus then rose from the table, His handsome countenance clouded with profound sadness. All eyes were on Him as He

---

[12] Luke 22:16
[13] John 14, 15, 16
[14] John 6:54
[15] Matt. 26:26-29; Mark 14:22-25; Luke 22:17-20

proceeded to remove His outer garment and gird Himself with a towel about His waist. They watched in perplexed wonder as He poured water into a basin and approached the first Apostle, commencing to wash his feet and wiping them dry with the towel.

In silent humility their Master went to each Apostle, until it was Simon Peter's turn. *"Lord, are you going to wash my feet?"* the Apostle objected. Jesus answered, *"You do not know now what I am doing but later you will understand."* But Peter, determined to take the towel and wash the feet of His beloved Lord instead, continued to remonstrate, *"You will never wash my feet."* With solemn compassion, Jesus looked up into the eyes of the impetuous fisherman and gently responded: *"Unless I wash you, you will have no share with me"*. In deep consternation Simon Peter quickly cried out: *"Lord, not only my feet, but also my hands and my head."* A quick smile crossed the face of the Incarnate Son before He solemnly told Peter: *"One who has bathed does not need to wash, except for the feet, but is entirely clean. And you are clean."*

Then turning to the other Apostles, Jesus added grimly, *"But not all of you"*; for being in the knowledge of all things He knew that Judas Iscariot, one of His own and seated at the table, would betray Him that very night.[16]

The hushed silence remained in that small upper room while their Master finished His humble ceremony, each of the Twelve continuing to watch in troubled awe.

Having regained His outer garment, Jesus returned to His seat at the table and addressed their puzzled expressions. *"Do you know what I have done to you?"* He said. *"You call me Teacher and Lord; and you are right, for that is what I am. If I then, being your Lord and Master, have washed your feet, you also ought to wash one another's feet. For I have set you an*

---

[16] John 13:4-11

example, so that you may also do as I have done to you. Truly I tell you, the servant is not greater than his master and neither is the apostle greater than He who sent Him. If you know these things, you shall be blessed if you obey me."[17]

Pausing to look around the table, gravely the Son of Man continued, "*I speak not of all of you for I know whom I have chosen. But that the Scriptures may be fulfilled, he who has eaten bread with me will this very night betray me.*"[18] Bewildered, the Apostles looked around at one another, all talking at once, not wishing to believe the shocking words.

Simon Peter whispered to John as to who it could be, and John, seated closest to the Master, queried of Him, "*Lord, who is it?*" Gently, Jesus confided: "*It is he to whom I shall give the dipped bread*". And when He had dipped the bread, the Son of Man reached over and gave it to Judas Iscariot, saying to him quietly, "*That what you have to do, do quickly*". The few others who heard, knew not to what purpose Jesus had said these words but to their innocent thinking that perhaps, because Judas held the purse-strings, their Master had wanted him to go out and purchase those things which were needed for the following feast day or that he should give something to the poor. Having taken the morsel, Judas left the room.[19]

With grievous sorrow, the Son of God lifted His eyes to Heaven, and prayed aloud: "*Father, the hour is come. Glorify thy Son that thy Son may glorify Thee; as You have given Him power over all flesh that He may give eternal life to all whom You have given Him. Now this is eternal Life: that they may know Thee, the only true God, and Jesus Christ whom Thou hast sent. I have glorified Thee on the earth; I have finished the work which You gave me to do. And now glorify me, O Father, with Thyself, with the glory which I had, before the world was, with*

---

[17] John 13:12-17
[18] John 13:18-21
[19] John 13:26-30

Thee."[20] Each of the Eleven heard the sweet words of affirmation.

In growing consternation, they then watched as their beloved Jesus bowed His head, saying quietly, *"The hour is now come"*. A deathly hush ensued.

Before rising, the Messiah solemnly looked around the table. With slow deliberation He told them they would all desert Him that night, just as it was written in the Scriptures that *the* S*hepherd would be struck and the sheep of His flock scattered."*[21] Promptly Simon Peter hotly remonstrated that he would never abandon His Lord and Master. Again, Jesus smiled at his impetuosity, *"Truly I tell you, Peter, this night, before the cock crows twice, you will have denied me three times."*[22] Then with compassion for the chastened and troubled Apostle, Jesus gently addressed them all, *"Yet although you will abandon me, I am never alone because the Father is with me."* And He continued quietly, *"These things I have told you, that in me you may have peace. In the world you will have distress: but have confidence, I have overcome the world."*[23]

So saying, the Son of Man stood up from the table, and with a deepening sense of foreboding the Eleven rose with Him. Together they followed Jesus out into the quiet of the moonlit night to the Mount of Olivet[24] for the Divine Son to pray to His Father in Heaven that all may be fulfilled.

---

[20] John 17:1-5
[21] John 16:32
[22] Mark 14:30
[23] John 16:32-33
[24] Matt. 26:30

Alone in the dim lighting of her small room, Mary remained on her knees, sharing in her heart the grievous pain her beloved Son was already enduring.

Dear Mary, Mother of Light,
May I be inspired and guided by your holy example
to have Faith and be comforted by Christ's miraculous Gift to us
of Himself in the Holy Eucharist.

Chapter 12

Jesus meets Mary on the Way of the Cross

W hat indescribable anxiety Mary suffered that night. Knowing as she did that her Divine Son had gone to His Last Supper with the Apostles, and, close as she was to Him, she was aware of the terrible spiritual agony He underwent thereafter in the Garden of Gethsemani on Mount Olivet[1] - to the point of sweating droplets of His Most Precious Blood as He prepared Himself to fulfill His final work of redemption on earth.

In the late evening, she heard how Judas Iscariot had come with a great multitude of soldiers to the Garden and in the darkness of that night had betrayed his Master with a kiss.[2] How distressed in her heart that one of His own should betray Him. She heard too how Peter had drawn out a nearby sword to defend his Master, striking out at the servant of the high priest and cutting off his ear. Simon Peter, the head-strong one, fiercely loyal and impetuous. Jesus had gently admonished him, telling him to put the sword back and adding, *"for all who take the sword will perish by it. Do you not know that I have only to ask of my Father, and He would give me more than twelve legions of angels? But how then shall the Scriptures be fulfilled?"*[3] And to the possible chagrin of those who had come to apprehend Jesus, her Divine Son had then promptly restored the ear of the writhing servant,[4] such was the great compassion and mercy of Christ even in His darkest moments.

Then, in meekness to the will of the Eternal Father, the Son of God had humbly surrendered Himself to His captives to be led away to Caephas the high priest, where the scribes and the elders were assembled. It was at that point that the Apostles had

---

[1] Luke 22:44; Matt. 26:36-45
[2] Luke 22:47
[3] Matt. 26:53
[4] Luke 22:51

fled into the night,[5] John to impart the grievous news to the Blessed Mother, to comfort her and stay with her throughout the long ordeal that inevitably lay ahead.

Simon Peter, they later learned, had followed the cohort from afar, and even ventured into the courtyard of the high priest, where he sat with the servants that he might know and report back to Mary and the others what had happened to her beloved Son. Angrily he perceived the chief priests and the whole Council seeking false witness against Jesus that they might put Him to death; one false witness after another came forward. Eventually Peter heard the high priest say to Jesus, *"Are you the Messiah, the Son of the Blessed One?"* and then his Master's quiet affirmation, *"I am; and you will see the Son of Man seated at the right of the Power and coming from the clouds of Heaven."* At this, the high priest shrieked *"Blasphemy!"* and grabbed at Jesus' handspun garment, ripping it.[6] The tension in the courtyard rose to a palpable crescendo. Helplessly Peter watched as they spat in his Master's face, punched and kicked Him, struck His face, mocked and scorned Him. The hot-headed Peter was having a tough time controlling his justifiable anger at the outrageous false accusations and atrocious treatment of his beloved Lord. A servant maid, noticing the Apostle's manner, accosted him, saying: *"You also were with Jesus, the Galilean".*[7] Promptly Peter denied it and hastily moved away toward the gates of the courtyard. At the gates, yet another servant recognized him, calling out *"This man was with Jesus of Nazareth".*[8] Again he denied it, and moved still further away to outside of the gates, where he mingled with the crowds gathered there, determined to glean information of what was going on inside the courtyard. But a man nudged him, saying *"Surely you are one of them; for you are a Galilean."*[9]

---

[5] Matt. 26:56
[6] Matt. 26:58-65
[7] Matt. 26:69
[8] Matt. 26:71
[9] Matt. 26:73

Annoyed that he should have been discovered yet again and anxious to stay a while longer, Peter's hot temper got the better of him and he vehemently began to curse and to swear that he knew not the Man. At that moment, in the far distance, he heard a cock crow for the second time and suddenly the Apostle remembered the words of his Master at the Last Supper that *before the cock crows twice, you will deny me three times.* Ashamed, Peter went out into the night and wept bitterly.[10]

Come morning, before the sun had risen in intensity, the Blessed Virgin, with John and Mary Magdalen, found themselves outside the gates of the Praetorium, anxious to know what had happened to their beloved Jesus. Through the multitudes that had assembled there, they squeezed their way to the outskirts of an inner arena where they heard the Messiah had been taken to be scourged.[11] Roman scourgings they knew, typically involved being whipped with a cat-of-nine-tails, which had bits of glass and metal tied to the ends, causing chunks of flesh to be ripped off the body, leaving wide open wounds. Choking sobs welled up within the gentle Mother when she heard the grim news. As they moved closer to the entrance of the arena, they could perceive in the distance, beyond the crowds, the high-arc wheeling of several whips and to their sensitive ears came the terrible, hideous sound of a brutal scourging. It seemed to go on and on without any pausing. Crushed and devastated, Mary crumpled to her knees. What manner of punishment was this? Surely they could beat her Divine Son no more - surely He had suffered enough at the hands of His cruel torturers.

But the sound continued. Loud and clear it echoed through the stone arched portals. Whoosh-crack-Whoosh-crack. Harder and faster that ugly horrendousness seemed to come. And at every crack of those torturous whips, the gentle Mother could

---

[10] Matt. 26:58-75; Mark 14:30; Mark 14:72
[11] Matt. 19:1

hear guttural jeers and hollow laughter. Surely His persecutors could not be enjoying such an abysmal and odious task! Mary could feel herself swooning - sickened by the vicious sounds - her broken heart wrenched and shattered at the abominable torture her precious Son was enduring. How much more pain and suffering must He determine to bear in order to atone for all the sins of the world! Oh that the lashings would cease. In vain the strong arms of John and loving words of Mary Magdalen tried to sustain her; their hearts, too, torn asunder, their faces smudged and tear-stained, stricken with their own intense grieving.

Then came silence. That frightful sound of the lashings was suddenly no more. Even those around them were silent as they steadily broke up and drifted away. To the crouched and weeping trio, time stood still in a chamber of unfathomable horror. Gently John helped the devastated and shaking Mother to her feet. Dreading to see what she might see, she instinctively looked up. Through the arched entranceway to the deserted arena, what she beheld brought her again to her knees. What excruciating brutality to bring about such a voluminous loss of her Divine Son's Precious Blood. It flowed in rivulets across the saturated ground and gleamed in the sunlight; a ghastly trail leading from the scene where His battered body had been dragged away. Surely Jesus could not have survived such a terrible scourging. Yet Mary knew it did not end there; the dread of what was now happening to her beloved Son consumed the gentle Virgin with a further tortured anxiety.

Even as she grappled with her own interior suffering, from the distance her ears picked up a rising noisiness and hubbub. Moved into action, the distraught Mother, with John and Mary Magdalen at her side, anxiously caught up to a tumultuous gathering now assembled at the outskirts of the blockaded arena of Pilot's inner court. From within came the heated tone of an even greater uproar which appeared to be growing uglier and angrier; through their terrible rage a dreadful chanting could be heard above the din, *"Crucify him, Crucify him".*[12] Ever stronger grew that frightful sound, the noise turning into a satanic frenzy. To the gentle Virgin, the words, as they gathered in ghastly momentum, carried the doom of Isaias' words[13] and Simeon's prophecy.[14] A cataclysmic grief overcame her, like a knife, wrenching and twisting into her very soul.

Then, incredibly, the tone of the crowd seemed to alter as though their lust for blood had been appeased. But even greater came that sickening feeling of dread within the soul of the weeping Mother. The gates to the Praetorium swung slowly open and the sound of the uproar again rose to a crescendo. A seething throng of bodies poured forth accompanied by Roman soldiers, their pointed plumed helmets and lofty spearheads oscillating vicariously through the crowds, the sun glistening off their metal shields and breastplates like sharp pinpricks of brilliant light. Instinctively Mary knew her beloved Son to be the focal point within their brutal midst. She must reach Him somehow - if only she could protect and shield Him as in the days of His infant Childhood.

In vain the devastated trio battled to pierce that intense wall of oncoming ferociousness, now cramming the narrow street that led out of the city toward Calvary. The Blessed Virgin clung desperately to John, tall gentle giant as he struggled through the crowds; behind her remained Mary Magdalen, holding fast to the sleeve of her robe, the three moving together as one. Gradually they were joined by others: the men clearly distressed, the women sobbing. Close against the rocky wall that skirted that side of the highway, they inched their way along, oblivious of the intense jostling and shoving and pushing, intent only on reaching their beloved Jesus. Steadily the array of swaying weaponry crept nearer, and as it did so, came too that hollow, gruesome sound of the wheeling and cracking of a whip

---

[12] John 19:6; Mark 15:13-14; Luke 23:21
[13] Psalm 21:13-19; Isaias 50:6
[14] Luke 2:33

amidst jeers and raucous laughter that came rippling toward the horror-stricken Mother in all their ugly enormity.

Closer and louder came those menacing sounds. Mary could now see the object of their cruel ridicule - her Divine and Blessed Son. Crushed by the weight of a grossly heavy cross-beam, her devastated eyes perceived His flagging and broken body as He swayed to and fro, held up only by the ropes that secured His arms to the patibulum, the free rope ends being yanked and pulled upon by his cruel oppressors. At His approach, both Mother and Son's eyes were destined to meet in an excruciatingly agonized moment. Ah what terrible torture – the Son to perceive His Mother's inconsolable grief; the Mother to perceive the shockingly gruesome persecution of her Son. Like so many daggers piercing those two beloved Hearts. In that same instant, Mary's eyes beheld the ripped and bloodied handspun garment, hanging loosely from her Son's sagging frame, and around His precious head a cruel crown of spiked thorns.[15] Down His face and heavily matted hair coursed a steady flow of blood as the thorns drove their way into His skull; His eyes puffed up and swollen, His precious countenance totally covered by openly bleeding wounds and gashes. Only the tender loving look in His eyes remained recognizable. And in that brief exchange did the Divine Son console His agonized Mother, such a look of indescribable Love and Compassion didst emanate from that one Godly glance.

From that moment on, in spite of the saddened words Jesus addressed to the weeping women close by,[16] Mary knew His strength would be with her always, even as she heard that cruel sound of another lashing and saw her precious Son stumble and fall from yet another vicious blow. She would see this frightful tragedy to its bitter end, be there for her beloved Jesus, Incarnate Son of God, no matter what the pain would cost.

---

[15] John 19:5; Mark 15:17
[16] Luke 23:28-30

With a heavily laden heart, the Blessed Virgin clung to John and Mary Magdalen, as the three, borne along by the pressing crowd, made their agonized way along the path that would lead to the Divine Saviour's ignominious crucifixion and death on the Cross.

Dear Mother, Courageous and Persevering,
May I be inspired and guided by your holy example
to bear all my crosses with Strength, Resignation and Patience.

Chapter 13

Crucifixion and Death of Jesus

Can anyone imagine what torturous sorrow - what heart-wrenching, soul-destroying pain the Mother of Christ suffered that fateful day of Our Blessed Lord's Passion, Crucifixion and Death.

First, that part of His Passion, the long cruel climb to Calvary - seeing Jesus so maliciously treated along that Sorrowful Way - His persecutors pulling and yanking on the ropes that held Him fast to the heavy cross-beam - His mutilated body being thrashed again and again by the cruel whips as He stumbled and fell, struggling to get up, only to fall again - blood seeping through every inch of His ripped garment and coursing like rivers down His precious face - His eyes swollen and bruised - His countenance unrecognizable so badly had He been beaten. Ah, could any mother look upon such torture to her own son and not be frantically tormented by an unspeakable grief and heartache.

Like a reed crushed in the wind, the Virgin Mary, together with her faithful comforters, continued to be borne along in the wake of the masses, most pushing and shoving in their macabre mania to witness the inevitable finality of Pilate's unjust sentencing; others though, like herself and John and Mary Magdalen, bewildered, devastated and sobbing.[1] In the distance they could just make out through the crowds, a big man now bearing the weight of that oppressively heavy cross-beam[2], while our beloved Saviour continued to stumble and fall, so weakened from the loss of blood and brutal handling by His vicious torturers. All along that rough, stony Way in the blazing heat of Jerusalem's midday sun, the Blessed Mother's ears could pick out the Whoosh-Crack of those cruel lashings as Jesus was

---

[1] Luke 23:27
[2] Luke 23:26; Matt. 27:32; Mark 15:21

forced to pick Himself up and drag His weary, pain-racked body to continue the arduous journey, accompanied by the raucous laughter and sadistic jeers. If only she could make His persecutors stop - reach out to Her Son with water to ease His parched throat and burning lips - wipe away the blood from his blinded eyes - remove that cruel band of piercing thorns around His precious head - nurse Him in her arms - comfort and console Him.

Would this long drawn out, pitiless torturing of her Son never end? Yet in the distance, through her tears she could just make out the notorious Hill of Golgotha - recognizable by its macabre sprinkling of crucifixions. Heavier and heavier did her heart sink with the dawning of the gruesome outcome that lay ahead. The devastated Mother could feel the road's gradient growing steeper, and as it did so, it seemed the sound of the lashings became more persistent, the shoutings of her Son's persecutors louder and angrier.

Finally, the mob came to a halt. They had reached the summit of Calvary, infamous Hill of Golgotha. A chilling silence fell upon the crowd. It was then that Mary beheld Jesus, His bruised and battered body now lying prostrate under the scorching sun, the brutal crown of thorns still firmly planted across His scalp. The guttural jeerings persisted as two soldiers gripped His bloodied garment and with one sweeping movement, stripped it away in one piece, leaving her Divine Son's precious body exposed to the mocking onlookers. To see her Son so shamefully stripped, persecuted, and humiliated was more than Mary could bear. She crumpled to her knees, briefly losing consciousness.

But that momentary oblivion could not halt the horrific progress of the inevitable fate being played out that day. With instant impact, the distraught Mother was aroused by the terrifying thud of heavy metal on steel. That abominable sound brought with it the immediate realization that her precious Son was suffering the cruelest of all tortures, a Roman crucifixion.[3] Ah how could her beloved Jesus withstand any more such torturous cruelty and excruciating pain, and how could the gentle Mother endure any more such inconsolable heartache. At each brutal blow of the hammer Mary's mind reeled back into oblivion, the abysmal, cataclysmic grief again and again cutting into her heart like a knife, tearing, wrenching and searing its way into her soul.

When next Mary beheld her Son, He was transfixed to that ignominious wooden Cross, blood flowing down its vertical beam from the ugly wounds in His tender feet so ruthlessly spiked to the grain. His arms, outstretched and twisted, were equally nailed to the horizontal, His Precious Blood cascading along their length and dripping steadily to the ground below. Already His newly girthed loincloth was saturated by the flow, as was the surrounding earth at the foot of the Cross.

Amazingly, the soldiers close at hand were oblivious of their vicious brutality. Vaguely the Immaculate Virgin became aware of them, loudly arguing amongst each other, their coarse and filthy language defiling the air with its impurity, blasphemy and vulgarity. Later Mary was to learn that their heated words were over her Son's clothing which they had ripped into four pieces and divided amongst themselves; the handspun robe she had so lovingly woven for Jesus they had left intact and were casting lots over it – thus in fulfillment of the Scriptures, *they have parted my garments among them, and upon my vesture they have cast lots.*[4]

The sobbing Mother could only continue to drag her tear-filled eyes upward to look into the precious face of her beloved Jesus, His eyes sealed by the flow of blood from the malicious ring of thorns. She perceived His body, hanging limp and distorted on that infamous Cross, a crude plaque affixed above

---

[3] Matt. 27:31; Mark 15:25; John 19:16
[4] Matt. 27:35; Mark 15:24; Luke 23:34; John 19:23-24

His dear head with the letters "INRI" (Jesus of Nazareth King of the Jews) inscribed in Greek, Latin, and Hebrew.[5] His entire body had been flailed beyond recognition so badly had He been beaten and bruised; His flesh hung in ribbons.

All around the gentle Virgin could hear the continuing cruel jeers[6] of the soldiers and others standing by, ignorant that they were mocking their Redeemer, the Messiah, the very Son of God. Could they not see Who they were abusing? Had they not heard His loving words, cried out earlier to His Father in Heaven, *"Father, forgive them, for they know not what they do"*?[7] Did they not wonder at the words of the desolate robber crucified alongside her Divine Son, who, after rebuking the blasphemy of the crucified thief on the other side of Christ, had turned to Jesus and begged, *"Lord, remember me when you come into your Kingdom"* - and the compassionate response of her Divine Son, *"Amen I say to you, this day you will be with me in Paradise"*.[8]

Again and again Mary crumpled to her knees, oblivious of the sharp stones, aware only of the torture her beloved Jesus was undergoing.

Agonizing minute after interminable hour slowly dragged on. Strong arms held on to the Virgin and vaguely she heard the soft words of John as he tried in vain to comfort and sustain her, and the loving words of her own sister-in-law (Mary of Cleophas), and those of Mary Magdalen and Salome (mother of the Sons of Zebedee) who were also now gathered at the feet of Christ.[9] Oh dear Father in Heaven, will you not now call your beloved Son Home? How much more suffering would Jesus be determined to undergo to save the world?

---

[5] Luke 23:38
[6] Mark 15:29-32
[7] Luke 23:34
[8] Luke 23:39-43
[9] John 19:25

Overhead clouds started gathering, steadily blotting out the fierce sun. A biting wind sprang up, whipping its way up the Hill of Golgotha, tearing away at the crucified Lord and other forlorn bodies hanging on their gruesome mounts. The sorrowing Mother longed to hold her beloved Jesus, unaware of her own steadily chilling discomfort. Duller and darker grew the overhead sky, the clouds gathering in momentum, crushing out the light and filling the air with a heightened sense of doom.[10] The crowds started breaking up and scattering, many afraid as an ominous silence settled over Calvary's hilltop.

From His high perch below the troubled sky, came the gentle voice of Jesus, clearly audible above the increasing wind. Tenderly His words addressed His Mother, *"Woman, behold thy son"*. And to the stalwart figure of John below, Jesus lovingly directed, *"Behold thy Mother"*.[11] Amidst His pain and torture, such compassion and caring in those, the Son of Man's final moments.

As Mother and adopted son held to each other, that final hour grew ever darker and stormier, thunder and lightening flashed across the heavens in alarming display, lighting up the tortured body of our cherished Saviour in its short bursts of energy. Suddenly they heard Jesus cry out to His Father in Heaven, *"My God, My God, why hast thou forsaken me?"*[12] Ah could ever there be a greater anguish? What excruciating isolation did the humanity of Christ suffer in His taking on the sins of the world. Wretchedly, His devastated Mother gazed upward, helpless and heartbroken, longing to envelop her Son in loving embrace, take away His torture and misery, comfort and console Him.

Interminable minutes passed on agonizingly as Mary continued to look on - powerless to do anything but to watch

---

[10] Mark 15:33
[11] John 19:26-27
[12] Mark 15:34; Matt. 27:46

and to wait for the fulfillment of her Divine Son's Holy Will. Then again, from the depths of His soul, she heard her Beloved cry out, *"I thirst"*.[13] Doubtless, Mary knew and understood Christ's thirst for those souls that would remain lost, but a centurion standing by, understanding not but perhaps moved to pity, hastily soaked a sponge in brine, and spearing it to the end of a lengthy lance, rushed forward with it, shoving it roughly into the lacerated and bleeding mouth of her precious Son. Dimly did Mary hear the mocking mutterings around her, *"Stay, let us see if Elijah will come to take him down"*.[14]

Even as her woeful eyes took in that final grim act so did the stormy skies rage ever more ferociously. The weeping Mother and chosen Apostle beheld their Beloved looking up into the flashing lightening, and above the violent noise of the crashing thunder, heard His loud cry, *"Father, it is consummated.[15] Into thy hands I commend my spirit"*.[16]

As His words were torn away on the wind, the Blessed Virgin Mary sorrowfully perceived her Divine Son's precious head fall to His chest in loving submission to the Eternal Father.

Dear Mary, Mother of Sacrificial Suffering,
by your holy Martyrdom,
May I find Inspiration and Strength
to die unto self for love of my Lord and Saviour.

---

[13] John 19:28
[14] Mark 15:35-36
[15] John 19:30
[16] Luke 23:46

Chapter 14

Jesus is Taken down from the Cross
and Laid in His Mother's Arms

How the heavens raged and tormented that historical afternoon of Our Blessed Lord's death on that infamous gibbet. Across the skies, thunder roared and crashed in deafening peels; lightening flashed in brilliant display illuminating the darkened universe in short bursts of blinding energy; the wind, whipped up to a howling frenzy, roared like a mighty dirge.

Crouched below the Cross, the weeping Mother in the arms of John, was oblivious of the electrifying display overhead; her senses dulled and numbed; she could only look up into the illuminated lifeless gaze of her beloved Son as the flashes of lightening cast a ghostly glow over His sunken countenance. At every flash from the heavens, she could perceive His twisted, broken body, hanging motionless, slumped forward from the cross-beam, held precariously by the rough nails and tightly-bound ropes, swaying in the onslaught of the mighty wind; around His precious Head, the sharp spiked thorns silhouetted against the intermittently illuminated skies.

Only vaguely could she hear the distant weeping and wailing, borne along the wind, of the group of women, sheltering in the distance; only vaguely was she aware of the lonesome, forlorn figures hanging crucified, one on either side of Jesus; the occasional Roman guard standing nearby. Time for her stood still, held in a capsule of desolate misery and wretchedness, her heart torn into tiny fragments of inconsolable grief. No words of comfort from John could console or sustain her; only dimly did she sense his presence and feel his strong arms holding on to her.

For some time Mary and John remained at the foot of the Cross, when, through the shrouded mist of that stormy afternoon, the sorrowing Virgin's attention was momentarily caught by the sight of a Roman centurion looming out of the darkness, his spiked helmet and metal tunic piercing the gloom, lit up in grim detail by the occasional flashes of brilliant light. In his hand he held a lance, its tall pointed peak rising high aloft. He approached the suspended figure of Jesus and in an instant, with one vicious blow, he drove the point of his spear into the side of her beloved Son.

Like one in an appalling nightmare, Mary watched in wide-eyed, abject horror as the soldier struggled to release the embedded spearhead from bondage. Shocked and sickened, she could not withdraw her stunned gaze from the brutal desecration.

A further flash of white light unexpectedly gave witness to its sudden liberation - and there poured forth from the open wound, both blood and water[1] - the ultimate outpouring of the Most Precious Blood of our Redeemer in the complete sacrifice of Himself for our sins; and did not the water flowing from the side of Christ signify His Gift of Baptismal washing to bring us back to new life with God.

In that final moment, then did the clouds surrender their mighty downpour, dropping in straight curtains of voluminous water, drowning the earth in teeming rivulets and bearing with it the most Precious Drops of Blood down the Hill of Golgotha and into oblivion. Vaguely Mary perceived the centurion on his knees in incredulous wonder as he cried out *"Indeed this was the Son of God"*,[2] his sorrowful moans almost drowned by the deafening outbreak of that raging storm.[3] The air became filled with the sound of loud cries and screams as the very ground shook and vibrated,[4] the anger of Nature ferociously giving vent

---

[1] John 19:33-37
[2] Matt.27:54
[3] Mark 15:54
[4] Matt. 27:51

in all its mighty fury. Fear held its own in that awesome and terrifying tempest.

Gently John lifted the desolate Mother from the sodden ground, leading her to nearby shelter where her sister-in-law Mary of Cleophas[5] (mother of James and Jude, Simon and Joseph), Mary Magdalen, and Salome mother of John and James (sons of Zebedee)[6] were there to comfort and console her, combining their heartbroken tears and sobbings with those of the inconsolable Virgin.

Then through the storm appeared one, Joseph of Arimathea[7] and with him Nicodemus,[8] offering to assist with the taking down of the precious body of Jesus from that ignominious wooden Cross. And when the wild raging finally tempered, the small group of devoted followers, under the intermittent softened flashings of lightening, erected long ladders, earlier conveyance for Roman cruelty, and tenderly, with great love and caring, took down the blessed body of Jesus and gently laid Him in Mary's waiting arms.

Ah could ever there be a greater pain for that loving Mother to look down at the crushed and desecrated body of her Incarnate Son, so cold and lifeless in her arms. Washed clean by the might of the Eternal Father, His broken body lay mutilated and lashed, His arms and legs dislocated, His skin hanging in ribbons from that cruel and vicious scourging, an ugly shoulder wound lacerated and wide-open from the heavy weight of the cross-beam; the mournful lighting revealing naked bone beneath the open flesh wounds - not one portion of the Son of Man's precious face or body had been left untouched and unviolated.

---

[5] Matt.13:55
[6] John 19:25, Matt. 27:56
[7] Matt. 27:57-58
[8] John 19:38-39

In silent anguish and horror, His weeping disciples encircled Mother and Son in loving embrace, their tears mingling in profusion together to flow over the precious body of our loving Saviour in unspeakable, inconsolable lamenting.

Dear Mary, Mother Most Devastated,
May I be inspired and guided by your holy example
to stalwartly accept the Will of God
and trust in His Strength to carry me through.

97

Chapter 15

Burial of Jesus

Some time after the soldiers had abandoned their vigil that tempestuous late afternoon, the storm gradually abated. Like the weepings of a spent child, the Heavens played out the last of their tearful tribute; the rolling thunder becoming a distant muffled rumble; the lightening, a gentle flashing at irregular intervals, illuminating the lifeless bodies hanging limply along the line of crucifixions that broke the dark horizon. Like a mournful wailing, the wind moaned its refrain across that lonesome hilltop.

Far below, under the dark canopy of those angry black clouds, remained the small group surrounding Mother and Son; the Blessed Virgin, her tear-filled eyes gazing helplessly up to Heaven, holding in her arms the cold, motionless body of her precious Son. Could ever a picture depict more heart-wrenching sorrow and unspeakable anguish than that lonely spectacle.

Gently, with the greatest of loving care, tender hands lifted the lifeless body of Jesus from His Mother's arms and struggling against the biting wind of that ominous storm, between them they solemnly carried their Beloved to a nearby tomb, hewn out of stone, one that had never been used before, owned by Joseph of Arimathea.[1]

Once inside that sacred shelter, the somber silence was complete. The sepulcher had already been prepared with an array of burning candles, offering a safe haven of light and warmth from the troubled dark skies overhead. Gently, loving hands then lifted the precious body on to the low, flat, stone plinth - final resting place of our beloved Lord Jesus Christ.

---

[1] John 19:38-39

Like one in a trance, the devastated Virgin Mary stared numbly at the sight of her Divine Son's desecrated body, now dimly lit by the flickering candle-light, ghastly in all the enormity of that violent and excruciating maltreatment. Tears continued to flow in a steady stream down her lovely face, her dark luminous eyes filled with an immeasurable depth of sadness. The redemptive work of our Saviour now fulfilled, her lonely and devastated soul longed to be enjoined with her Son Incarnate.

It was hard to believe that only days before she had sat quietly listening to Jesus, His beautiful face aglow under another flickering candle-light as Mother and Son had shared time together in the quiet of the evening, the voice of Jesus soft and gentle, yet strong and vibrant when addressing the thousands who flocked to hear His every Word; His eyes, so tender and compassionate, filled with the joy of Life itself; His loving presence filling every corner of every room, and reaching far out into the crowds, who would gather in their droves just to be with Him and follow wherever He might go. Precious memories of her beloved Jesus filled the gentle Virgin's soul with a bitter sweet anguish, and back again came the prophetic words of Simeon[2] – now played out in their sorrowful finality.

Steadily the pungent smell of myrrh and aloe pervaded the tiny chamber. The Blessed Mother became aware of the quiet activity around her and, quickly, mechanically, she joined with them in the loving anointing with spices and binding of the precious body with fresh linen cloths in the initial preparation of burial according to Jewish custom.[3] And all the while, in that dimly lit room, the somber silence remained complete, broken only by an occasional stifled sob, the atmosphere filled with an intense, indescribable sadness.

---

[2] Matt. 2:34-35
[3] John 19:40-42

Finally, all initial preparations concluded, Mary stooped to gently kiss the now ice cold brow of her sweet Son in a final motherly gesture of heart-wrenching farewell. Then firm but gentle arms surrounded the Blessed Mother, assisting her faltering steps as they lovingly shepherded her out into the stormy darkness. A large stone was rolled across the entrance,[4] sealing the sacred burial place of our beloved Saviour. Then, slowly, sadly, His small band of devoted followers, surrounding the Blessed Virgin Mary, turned away into the forlorn bleakness of that dark lonesome eve of the Jewish Sabbath.

Dear Mother, Inconsolable and Grieving,
May I be inspired and guided by your holy example
to want never to be separated from my sweet Saviour.

---

[4] Mark 15:46

Chapter 16

The Resurrection

It was very early in the morning after the Sabbath, the dawning still a dim greyness. Gradually, like the unfurling of a new leaf, the shadowy foliage in the Garden took shape as the sun slowly lifted above the horizon. Birds were chirping and twittering as they hopped in and out of the leafy shrubbery, the air charged with the fresh smell of dew on wet grass and the sweet scent of fragrant bushes combined with that of almond, olive and pine.

In the peaceful quietude of that early hour came Mary Magdalen and several of the other women – devoted followers of Jesus, now referred to as the Holy Women,[1] walking quickly, their heads covered, in their arms alabaster jars of spices, aromatic oils and ointments. They had come to make the final burial preparations for their sweet Lord. As they entered the Garden they felt the ground shudder at their feet[2] and on approaching the sepulcher where they had laid Him the third day previously, they paused to stare in abject alarm. For the heavy stone that had been placed over its entrance had been rolled away, and seated thereon was an angel, his countenance as bright as lightening, his raiment as white as snow; at his feet the guards who had been stationed at the entrance of the tomb, prostrate on the ground as though dead. In wide-eyed amazement the women stood gaping at the heavenly being who then spoke, his voice as musical instruments, *"Do not be afraid. You seek Jesus of Nazareth, who was crucified: He is risen, He is not here, see the place where they laid Him. But go, tell His disciples and Peter that He goes before you into Galilee. There you shall see Him, as He told you."[3]* At these words, the women turned and fled, not trusting what they had seen or

---

[1] Luke 24:10
[2] Matt. 28:2
[3] Mark 16:6-7, Matt. 28:2-6, Luke 24:5-9

heard,[4] fear giving wings to their flight, each thinking what they had seen to be a figment of her imagination.[5] They were only aware that their precious Lord and Master had been removed from His sacred tomb.

Mary Magdalen was the first to reach the house where she and the Virgin Mary, the other Holy Women and some of the Apostles were staying. Bursting through the door, she sobbed incoherently, *"They have taken away the Lord, out of the sepulcher."*[6] Simon Peter and John immediately rushed out of the house, with Mary Magdalen close on their heels.

The Blessed Mother remained behind, her heart bursting with joy, for, close to her Son as she was, she had had an unwavering faith that on the third day He would rise from the grave into new Life, just as He had promised[7] - and indeed, Tradition teaches that her Divine Son had already appeared to her before the dawning of that Sabbath morn. Returning to the quietude of her small room, Mary sank to her knees, continuing her prayerful communion with Almighty God.

In the meantime, the three disciples came running to the place where Jesus had been laid, John slightly ahead of the others. He paused at the entrance, too overcome to go into the tomb. Simon Peter, coming up behind him, stooped down and entered. He stared in amazement at the linen cloths and separate napkin that had been laid over the face of their Blessed Lord.[8] With his usual impulsiveness, he picked up the coverings and holding them close to his heart, ran out into the Garden to return home.

---

[4] Mark 16:8
[5] Luke 24:11
[6] John 20:2
[7] Mark 9:30; Luke 24:16; Matt.16:21
[8] John 20:3-7

John then hesitantly entered the empty tomb, scarcely believing the evidence of his own eyes, his mind racing with the words of his Master that *on the third day He would rise again.*[9] Through tears of joy, he turned and stumbled out into the early morning sunshine to tell the others that Christ was risen.[10]

Mary Magdalen now approached the entrance, tears streaming down her stricken face. Seeing the sepulcher unguarded, she stooped to peer in through the opening, and stared in mortified wonder. For seated one at the head and one at the foot where the body of Jesus had lain, she again beheld through her tears, not one but two angelic beings, their garments shining as the morning sun, lighting up the darkness of the empty cavern. In wide-eyed terror, she stared at them. *"Woman, why are you weeping?"* she heard them say. *"Because they have taken away my Lord; and I know not where they have laid Him,"* she stammered, turning to escape from the chamber. As she withdrew from the entrance, she vaguely became aware of a Man standing near at hand whom she thought to be the gardener. *"Woman, why are you weeping? Who are you looking for?"* He asked of her. Distraught and beside herself with grief, she blurted out, *"Sir, if you have carried Him away, tell me where you have laid Him, and I will take Him away."*[11]

"Mary!" the voice softly called her name. Stunned, Mary Magdalen lifted her tear-stained face to gaze in wonder at the Figure standing before her, for the voice she instantly recognized as that of Jesus. Rushing forward she joyfully cried out, *"Master!"* but tenderly Jesus halted her movement, saying, *"Do not touch me, for I am not yet ascended to my Father. But go to my brethren, and say to them: I am ascending to my Father and to your Father, to my God and your God."*[12]

---

[9] Matt. 16:21; Mark 9:30; Luke 24:16
[10] John 20:8
[11] John 20:11-15
[12] John 20:16-17

Then did her elation know no bounds. With uncontained excitement, Mary Magdalen tore through the Garden to relay the wondrous news to the others. *"I have seen the Lord!"*[13] she exclaimed joyfully. The household gathered around, eager to hear her every word, their excitement delighting the gentle heart of the Blessed Mother of God. However, not everyone was so ready to rejoice - for there were those who still doubted the glad tidings.[14]

Earlier in the morning of that same day, Cleophas and one other left the household and set off for Emmaus, a small town sixty furlongs from Jerusalem. As they walked along the road and talked together, a Man drew close and joined them, asking what they were talking about and why they looked so sad. They stared at Him incredulously, *"Are you the only stranger in Jerusalem who does not know the things that have taken place there in these days concerning Jesus of Nazareth, who was a prophet, mighty in work and word before God and all the people?"* and together they related to the Stranger how the chief priests and scribes had delivered Jesus to be condemned to death, and had crucified Him – the one disciple confessing sadly that they had hoped Jesus would be the one to redeem Israel; the other adding excitedly that this was the third day since these things had happened, and that some women of their group had gone to the tomb early that morning and when they did not find His body there, had reported they had seen a vision of angels who claimed that Jesus was alive![15]

Then the Stranger gently upbraided them, saying: *"O foolish, and slow of heart to believe in all that the prophets have declared. Was it not necessary that the Messiah should suffer these things and then enter into His glory?"* And beginning with Moses and all the prophets, with great knowledge and wisdom

---

[13] John 20:18
[14] Mark 16:11
[15] Luke 24:13-23

the Stranger pointed out to them all that was written in the Scriptures concerning the Son of Man.

As they drew nigh to the town, the Man was about to make His departure but the disciples invited Him to sup with them as evening was drawing nigh. When they sat at table, the Stranger took bread, blessed and broke it, and gave it to them. And immediately, by that single act, the disciples recognized the Stranger – it was Jesus, their Lord and Master! But in that same instant He vanished from their sight, leaving the two of them gaping. When finally they found their tongues, they said to one another, *"Were not our hearts burning within us while He was talking to us on the road, opening the Scriptures to us?"* Elated over the revelation and anxious to tell the others, the disciples promptly left Emmaus and headed back to Jerusalem.[16]

Arriving at the house, they found everyone gathered there, the doors locked for fear of those who had crucified our Saviour. While the two were enthusiastically relaying the events, to the astonishment of all, Jesus miraculously appeared among them. *"Peace be with you,"*[17] He addressed their wide-eyed wonder. *"It is I, do not be afraid,"* for there were still those who could not believe the evidence of their own eyes. But Jesus, knowing all things, calmed their fears as He softly spoke to them, *"Why are you troubled, and why do you doubt? See my hands and feet, that it is I myself; touch, and see: for a ghost does not have flesh and bones, as you see me to have."* And He showed them His hands and feet. They crowded about Him, touching His garment, His hands and His feet, all talking at once and filled with great excitement and awe.[18] His Blessed Mother stood among them, close to her beloved Son, her heart exploding with sheer joy and happiness.

---

[16] Luke 24:13
[17] John 20:19-20
[18] Luke 24:36-40

Later Jesus asked, *"Have you anything to eat?"* and He ate a piece of broiled fish and a honeycomb with them so that they might believe He was truly the Son of Man resurrected from the dead as He had promised and as foretold in the Scriptures. *"These are my words that I spoke to you while I was still with you, that everything written about me in the law of Moses, the prophets, and the psalms must be fulfilled."*[19] And He opened their minds to understand the holy Scriptures, saying: *"Thus it is written, that the Messiah is to suffer and to rise from the dead on the third day, and that repentance and forgiveness of sins should be preached in His name to all nations, beginning at Jerusalem. You are witnesses of these things."*[20]

Having reassured and comforted them, just as our sweet Saviour had unexpectedly appeared in their midst, so He mysteriously vanished. What wondrous rejoicing filled the household that night. Long into the late hours they talked and laughed and shared their great love for the Divine Son with His Blessed Mother.

The next day Thomas, one of the Eleven not with them when Jesus appeared, arrived at the door to be greeted by happy faces. *"We have seen the Lord,"* he heard their one accord. Thomas stared at the Blessed Virgin Mary and the others in bewilderment. He wanted to believe but what they were saying was too good to be true. *"Except I see in His hands the print of the nails, and put my finger into the place of the nails, and put my hand into His side, I shall not believe,"* he stoutly averred.

Eight days later, while Thomas was with them, although the doors were locked, Jesus suddenly appeared again in their midst. *"Peace be with you"*, He addressed their startled though joyful reaction. Thomas stared in wide-eyed amazement. *"Put your finger here and see my hands. Reach out your hand and put it in my side. Do not doubt, but believe!"* coaxed Jesus, but the

---

[19] Luke 24:41-44
[20] Luke 24:45-48

Apostle was already on his knees, ashamed at his disbelief. "*My Lord and my God*" he stammered. "*Have you believed because you have seen me, Thomas? Blessed are those who have not seen and yet have come to believe*" His Master gently chided.[21]

Dear Mary, Mother of Indomitable Faith,
May I be inspired and guided by your holy example
to believe in the Resurrection of our Risen Lord
and the Life of the world to come.

---

[21] John 20:24-29

Chapter 17

The Ascension

What heartfelt rejoicing for the Blessed Virgin Mary as she saw how the Eleven Apostles and other Holy Women shared in her joyous excitement over the evidence of her Risen Son. The days that followed were filled with sweet anticipation as they would wait for their beloved Master to appear again in their midst, filling the room with the precious Peace of His Holy Presence and the joy of His Holy Spirit.

One evening of special note, shortly after Jesus had first appeared in Jerusalem, Simon Peter left the house to go fishing, taking with him John, James, Thomas, Nathanael and two other Apostles. Later the following day, he shared with the Blessed Mother the events of that memorable occasion. They had pushed the heavy boat out into the Sea of Galilee, he told her; it was a beautiful night, the sea a mirrored calm, a perfect night for fishing. Yet, strive as they might, they had caught nothing.

Come early morning, as the sun peaked over the mountains in gold splendour, the tired fishermen pulled toward shore. The dark shape of a solitary Figure was standing on the wet sand. He called out to them, asking if they had caught any fish, His strong voice crossing the water in the crispness of the early morning air. When they had answered in the negative, the Stranger had called back, encouraging them to cast their net on the right side of the ship *"and you shall find."*

Anxious to make a catch and too exhausted to argue, they did as instructed and immediately their net filled with a multitude of fish, so great that the Apostles could not haul its weight back into their boat. Turning to Simon Peter, John had whispered, *"It is the Lord!"* Peter looked across at the Figure now crouched in the sand, and without further thought had jumped overboard into the water and began to swim the fifty meters or so toward Him, while the rest of the crew brought the ship close to shore dragging the heavy net alongside. As soon as they landed, they could see the Stranger had made a small fire, and in the early light of the dawn seemed to be cooking something over the hot coals. *"Bring some of the fish you have caught,"* He called to them.

Simon Peter by now had almost reached the shore and was straightening up from the water when his attention was caught by an apparent difficulty with the fishing net. He quickly splashed his way over to the crew to help drag it ashore; the net was loaded with a huge catch of at least one hundred and fifty fish he estimated. But remarkably the meshed webbing was not broken. They heard the solitary Figure calling again, *"Come and eat with me"* and this time, Peter confessed to Mary, each one of them joyfully then recognized their Lord and Master![1]

This was the third time Jesus had manifested Himself to His disciples after rising from the dead. Seated on the soft sand in the quiet beauty of that early morning, they happily camped around the small fire on the seashore, while Jesus gave them bread to eat and fish.

Once they had eaten, Jesus turned to Peter and quietly asked of him: *"Simon, son of Jona, do you love me more than these?"* Earnestly, Peter assured Mary, he had promptly responded, *"Yes, Lord, you know that I do"*. Then Jesus instructed him, *"Feed my lambs"*. At that point, all eyes were on the Messiah, who appeared to be quietly looking into the dying flames. Then He lifted His head and looking again at Peter, Jesus had repeated, *"Simon, son of Jona, do you love me?"* Again Simon Peter had responded, *"Yes Lord, you know that I love you"*. A second time Jesus instructed him: *"Feed my lambs"*. Another pause ensued. No one dared speak while Jesus continued gazing intently into the smoldering ashes. A third time, He looked up at Peter and said: *"Simon, son of Jona, do you love me?"* Peter

---

[1] John 21:1-12

was then deeply grieved, he woefully told the gentle Mother, for he realized it had been three times he had denied knowing his Lord before the cock had crowed at dawn in the courtyard of the high priest prior to the crucifixion of her Son. Anxious to confirm what he had previously denied, he had promptly responded with true fervour, *"Lord, you know all things: you know that I love you"*. And again Jesus firmly told him: *"Feed my sheep"*.[2]

Gently the Blessed Mother encouraged Peter to tell her more.

All seated in the sand around the dying embers that morning, Peter then confided, were reminded that Jesus had appointed him as the rock upon which He would build His Church. Jesus warned Peter that his role would not be an easy one, saying: *"Truly I tell you, when you were younger, you did gird yourself, and did walk where you would. But when you grow old, you will stretch forth your hands, and another will gird you and lead you where you won't want to go"*[3] signifying by what manner of death Peter would glorify God. With tender compassion the Virgin Mary looked upon the large frame of the humble fisherman seated before her, his head bowed for a moment in quiet humility before he continued the recounting.

"Follow me" he then heard Jesus saying. As Peter looked up he noticed John already following Jesus, and having caught up with them, he asked what manner of death John would suffer in order to glorify God. Jesus had gently replied, *"So what if I wish him to remain until I come, what is that to you? Follow thou me."*[4] Tenderly Mary took Peter's hand, her heart sharing his understanding of what her Son's words had meant. For indeed, while it would be Peter's onerous, and indeed dangerous role in such times to head up Christ's Church on earth, it would

---

[2] John 21:13-17
[3] John 21:18-19
[4] John 21:19-23

be John's more gentle and less dangerous responsibility to watch over and protect the Blessed Mother as Jesus had so instructed from the Cross.

After that eventful occasion at the Sea of Galilee, over a period of some forty days[5] after His crucifixion and death, Jesus appeared many times to His Mother and to the Eleven and the other Holy Women, continuing to instruct them, confirming His earlier teachings and establishing the foundation of His Church on earth. How special that time they spent with their beloved Lord and Master.

"Go out into the whole world and preach the gospel to every nation", Jesus instructed His Apostles. *"He who believes and is baptized will be saved: but he who does not believe will be condemned"*. And understanding the difficulty of such a task, our sweet Saviour comforted them saying, *"These signs shall follow those who believe: In my Name they will cast out devils; they will speak in new tongues; they will take up serpents; and if they drink of anything deadly, it will not harm them; they will lay their hands on the sick and they will recover"*.[6]

When finally it was time for His departure from this earth, our Risen Lord gently told His Mother and faithful disciples, gathered together in the upper room of the large house late one afternoon, that He must leave them now to rise up to Heaven to be seated at the right hand of His Father.[7] The Blessed Virgin knew and understood but many of His disciples were still perplexed, and all of them were sad.

As the sun began its gradual descent, they slowly made their way to Mount Olivet as Jesus had instructed, their hearts filled with a great heaviness. When they reached the summit, their beloved Master came and stood among them; tall and

---

[5] Acts 1:3
[6] Mark 16:14-18
[7] Mark 16:19

handsome, charging the air all around them with His omnipotent and awe-inspiring Presence – the late afternoon sun dipping slowly toward the horizon behind Him, outlining His majestic frame in golden splendour.

Turning first to His Eleven, Jesus cautioned them to stay in Jerusalem until they would shortly receive the promise of His Father in Heaven with which they would be imbued Power from on High;[8] *"for John indeed baptized with water, but you will be baptized with the Holy Ghost not many days hence"*[9] - which Gift would fortify them with the strength and wisdom, knowledge and understanding to enable them to go out and preach to all nations the Word of God.

Raising His hands, their Master then blessed each one of them,[10] reiterating: *"All power is given to me in Heaven and on earth. Go therefore, teach all nations; baptizing them in the name of the Father, and of the Son, and of the Holy Ghost; and teach them to observe all things that I have commanded you".*[11] In all humility the Apostles bowed their heads, for most had come from humble backgrounds and certainly were troubled at the prospect of such a daunting mission, especially after witnessing their Master's unjust crucifixion at the hands of the Romans. *"Lord, will you at this time restore the Kingdom to Israel?"* they anxiously asked. But Jesus gently replied: *"It is not for you to know the time or moment the Father has put in His own power - but you will receive the power of the Holy Ghost, coming down upon you, and you shall be my witnesses in Jerusalem, and in all Judea, and Samaria, and even unto the uttermost ends of the earth."*[12]

---

[8] Luke 24:49
[9] Acts 1:5
[10] Luke 24:50
[11] Matt. 28:18-20
[12] Acts 1:7-8

Then the Incarnate Son tenderly embraced His Mother, gently consoling her as He looked down into her somber tear-filled eyes. How that lowly Maiden's heart ached to go where her Jesus was going! Yet even as she looked up into the face she knew and loved so well, so did His Godly tenderness meet her gaze, comforting and strengthening her with the purity of His divine love.

Similarly, Jesus turned to console the other Holy Women who were present - each uncertain of what was to come but equally filled with an immeasurable sadness.

The final moment now come, the Son of Man stood facing His Blessed Mother, the silent group gathered about her - and addressing their saddened expressions, He comfortingly reassured them with His sweet promise *"Behold I am with you all days, even unto the consummation of the world."*[13] Long would the Blessed Virgin Mary and each of those assembled around her, remember those precious words and the loving, compassionate way Jesus looked upon them on that mountain top that last day they would see our Risen Lord.

And so saying, with His right hand held up in farewell gesture, Jesus raised Himself off the ground, and before their awe-struck eyes, ascended slowly upward into the fading blue skies. Sadly they watched in gaping wonder as their beloved Master continued His ascent into the Heavens above until a thick white cloud hid Him from their sight.[14]

Speechless, they continued to gaze up into the skies.

Suddenly there were two men, standing beside them in snowy white raiment, asking why they were looking up to Heaven and consoling them with the words, *"This Jesus who is*

---

[13] Matt. 28:20
[14] Acts 1:9

taken up from you into Heaven, will come again, as you have seen Him going into Heaven".[15]

Dear Mary, Mother of our Heavenly King,
May I be inspired and guided by your holy example
to strive and long for Heaven, my true Home.

---

[15] Acts 1:10-11

Chapter 18

Descent of the Holy Ghost

That late afternoon of the Ascension was a particularly glorious one, the sun setting beyond the horizon in resplendent gold fury, steadily turning the heavens from a brilliant ochre to deeper shades of magnificent amber. Yet Mary and each of her Son's devoted disciples, tearful at the final parting of their beloved Jesus, were unaware of the beauty of the sunset. They wordlessly made their way slowly down Mount Olivet, each wrapped in their own thoughts, dazed expressions clouding their countenances. Their hearts were filled with mixed reactions - wonderment at what they had just beheld - joy at the realization that our beloved Messiah had gone to His Father in Heaven - and sadness that they would no longer see Him in the flesh - yet comforted by the promise of our sweet Saviour that He would be with them always *even unto the consummation of the world*.[1]

Such words of reassurance are a reminder of the precious gift the Son Incarnate left for all of His penitent faithful - the gift of Himself in the Holy Eucharist; that miraculous transformation of ordinary bread into the holy Bread of Life Eternal, and wine into the Chalice of unending salvation - true Presence of Christ (His mystical Body, Blood, Soul and Divinity).[2] How like the Redeemer to leave the world with such a comforting miracle to strengthen us with His grace, peace and joy.

No matter what difficulties and hardships lay ahead for His faithful Mother and His devoted disciples, they each knew they could always rely on Christ's promise. By the time they had reached Jerusalem the gentle heart of Mary was already aglow with the fire of her Divine Son's comforting love. His dedicated followers, too, had found His peace and were now talking

---

[1] Matt. 28:20
[2] Matt. 26:26-29; Mark 14:22-25; Luke 22:17-20

animatedly amongst one another. John put a caring arm around his adopted Mother and smiling together they entered the big house with the others.

They climbed the stairs to the upper room, and with the other Holy Women already waiting, immediately knelt together in joyful prayer.[3] Group prayer would become a key element of their daily lives, for their loving Master had told them *"where there are two or three gathered together in my Name, there am I in their midst"*.[4] Before departing from them Jesus had also told them: *"I go to the Father: and whatever you ask of the Father in my Name, that I will do: that the Father may be glorified in the Son"*.[5] Sweet words of consolation not only for His Blessed Mother and His disciples, but also for the entire world.

And to those in any doubt, Jesus had confirmed: *"Do you not believe that I am in the Father and the Father in me? The words that I speak to you, I speak not of myself but the Father who abides in me."*[6] And again on a previous occasion: *"He who believes in me does not believe in me but in Him who sent me; and he who sees me, sees Him who sent me.[7] For I have not spoken of myself but the Father who sent me, He has commanded what I should say"*.[8]

Shortly after the Ascension the early Christians in Jerusalem numbered about one hundred and twenty.[9]

Simon Peter, easily recognized as the head of their growing Church,[10] addressed the Apostles one morning shortly after the Ascension, saying that it was time to elect a twelfth Apostle to

---

[3] Acts 1:12-14
[4] Matt. 18:20
[5] John 14:13
[6] John 14:10
[7] John 12:44-45
[8] John 12:49
[9] Acts 1:15
[10] Matt. 16:18

replace Judas, the one who had betrayed Jesus.[11] Indeed, word had been passed around that Judas Iscariot had become ashamed of his traitorous act and had tried to take back what he had done by returning the thirty pieces of silver to those whom he had later learned were plotting to put his innocent Master to death. But the chief priests and scribes would not accept the return of the blood money, and Judas, beside himself with misery, had then thrown the coins on to the ground before them and run out into the night. Tormented by guilt and filled with despair, he had gone to a lonely field and there hung himself from a tree. The field quickly became known as Haceldama, meaning The Field of Blood.[12] When Mary received the news, her heart was filled with a great sadness knowing that her Divine Son grieves over the loss of even one soul. If only Judas could have turned back to God with true remorse and repentance; had he not understood the saving message of his loving and forgiving Master?

So under Peter's leadership it was decided to elect two from the many who had been faithful followers of Jesus and to then cast lots to select which of the two would be the one to bring the number of the Chosen back up to Twelve. The two who were chosen were Joseph called Barsabas who was surnamed Justus, and Matthias.[13] Before casting lots, the Apostles then prayed: *"You, Lord, who know the hearts of all men, show which of these two you have chosen to take the place of the ministry and apostleship from which Judas has by transgression fallen"*. The lot fell upon Matthias, so that he became the twelfth Apostle.[14] This then set the precedent for appointing successors to the Discipleship, and indeed a similar precedent for the appointment of a successor to Simon Peter who was the first Bishop and also the first Pope of the early Church that Christ had instituted on earth.

---

[11] Acts 1:15
[12] Acts 1:18-20
[13] Acts 1:23
[14] Acts 1:24-26

Thus it was one quiet morning, some ten days after the Ascension, all Twelve were gathered together in the upper room of the big house, along with the Blessed Virgin Mary. It was a beautiful day, the sun shining brightly through the windows without a breath of air to stir the day's calm. As was their practice, they were assembled around the centre table, having prayed together and were now discussing amongst themselves no doubt the promise of our beloved Saviour that His Father would send to them the Holy Ghost, the Paraclete, in His name, to help the Apostles fully comprehend all that Jesus had taught them.[15]

There suddenly came a mighty sound as of a powerful gushing wind; it reverberated throughout the entire house, filling every corner with its immense ferocity. Wide-eyed alarm and perplexity crossed the faces of all around the table, and even as they exchanged bewildered looks, there appeared parted tongues as of the flame of a fire over the head of each of them.[16]

They were instantly filled with the Holy Ghost and with a complete understanding of the holy Scriptures and all that their Master had taught them - just as He had promised them.[17] And the Apostles found they each could speak in different languages with full comprehension of the various dialects,[18] precious gift to enable them to carry out their missionary work of bringing souls back to God; they were immediately inspired and strengthened to face the daunting prospect of the work ahead of them. In spite of the enormity of the moment, a profound Peace flowed through each heart in the room as the fire of God's loving Presence burned into the soul of each and every one of them. What sweet ecstasy for the Blessed Virgin to again experience the pure joy of her espoused Holy Ghost, reaffirming His great love for her.

---

[15] John 14:26
[16] Acts 2:3
[17] John 14:16-20
[18] Acts 2:1-4

That eventful day was the Jewish Feast of Pentecost, and on such a feast day God gave the Ten Commandments to Moses on Mount Sinai – God's Law written in stone at that time,[19] now written in the hearts of those whom He had baptized with His Holy Ghost.[20] What great joy for Mary to behold – her Divine Son's promise fulfilled in her humble presence. She looked around the table at the elated faces of her beloved Twelve and her heart swelled in grateful thanks to Almighty God for the wondrous gift of His Holy Spirit to mankind.

When the violent wind rocked the large house in Jerusalem, a multitude of devout men of every nation gathered outside - Parthians, Medes, Elamites, inhabitants of Mesopotamia, Judea, Cappadocia, Pontus and Asia, Phrygia, Pamphylia, Egypt, and the parts of Libya about Cyrene, and strangers of Rome, Jews and proselytes, Cretes, and Arabians.[21] For they had been filled with wonder and alarm at the velocity and ferocity of the wind which they had experienced elsewhere in the city and heard how it had rocked the large house. They noisily banged on the gates of the courtyard and called out to the occupants, feeling certain that the holy group within would understand its supernatural cause. From the upper windows, the gentle Virgin Mary and other Holy Women looked down on the amassing crowds with tender compassion. Simon Peter opened the gates to greet them, and when he spoke they were dumb-founded and amazed when they each heard him and the other Apostles speaking in their own native languages – these men whom they knew to be Galileans! And in that moment they knew the great wind to have come from the Almighty Hand of God.

Later, however, news reached the household that others were mocking the miracle, saying: *These men are full of wine*.[22] So Peter, no longer hesitant and fearful but filled with

---

[19] Ex. 31:18
[20] Jer. 31:33
[21] Acts 2:6-11
[22] Acts 2:13

the gifts of strength and knowledge from the Holy Ghost, stood up with the Eleven, and gave his first sermon to the people – firmly denouncing the claim of their drunkenness, and then going on to remind the people of Joel's prophecy, that God would show *wonders in the heaven above and signs on the earth beneath: blood and fire, and vapours of smoke; that the sun shall be turned into darkness, and the moon into blood, before the great and manifest day of the Lord come*[23] and encouraging them to call upon the name of the Lord and be saved.[24] He outlined the plan of God's salvation through Jesus Christ, exhorting them to save themselves from the perversity of their generation.[25] Listening to her beloved Peter's words, Mary felt a great joy over the Apostle's inspired preaching, glorifying her Jesus, the Son of God.

Many demanded to know what they could do to be saved. *"Do penance, and be baptized every one of you in the name of Jesus Christ, for the remission of your sins"*, Peter told them, *"and you will receive the gift of the Holy Ghost"*.[26] Not only was this a message for the early Christians, but a message for the entire world even today.

A great number of them were baptized and the early Church rapidly grew to some three thousand souls at that time.[27] For the Apostles, strengthened by the gifts of the Holy Ghost, fearlessly went forth as witnesses of the Divine Word, spreading the fire of God's love and promoting the Kingdom of God in the name of Jesus Christ.

Those days were happy ones and busy as the Blessed Mother and other Holy Women helped the Twelve to expand their Discipleship. They would continue to pray and sing hymns

---

[23] Acts 2:19
[24] Acts 2:20
[25] Acts 2:22-36
[26] Acts 2:37-38
[27] Acts 2:41

of worship and praise in the Temple, but for the Eucharistic Breaking of Bread they would gather together in private homes.[28] For the continuing work of the Apostles in converting, healing and casting out demons in the name of Jesus remained a concern to the chief priests and scribes who were disgruntled and angry that the crucifixion and death of Jesus did not deter nor diminish the Christian movement; they persisted in seeking ways to discredit the work of the Apostles. After their treatment of her Divine Son, Mary, along with the other Holy Women, were distressed over the rumours.

So the early Christians kept to themselves, becoming a close-knit, loving community. Their goods and possessions they sold, dividing them among one another according to need. They took their food with gladness and simplicity of heart, giving thanks to Almighty God and praising Him for His great goodness, and their numbers continued to grow.[29]

Dear Mother, devoted Spouse of the Holy Ghost,
May I be inspired and guided by your holy example,
to pray for the Gifts of the Holy Ghost in my own soul.

---

[28] Acts 2:46
[29] Acts 2:44-47

Chapter 19

The Assumption

Before the dawn had yet broken the early morning greyness, the Blessed Virgin Mary slipped quietly out of the house, walking quickly through the deserted streets of Jerusalem. It was her favourite time of the day, regularly taking the narrow street leading out of the city to the Hill of Golgotha, to tread the ground where her Incarnate Son had suffered what had become passionately known as His Way of the Cross. In the quiet of the grey light, she would take time to pause along its length, and pray, feeling the Presence of her precious Son as one at the graveside of a dearly beloved.

This particular morning, some several decades after the glorious resurrection of our loving Saviour, a swirling mist had gathered, a chilling wind accompanying the austere clouds overhead; a bleak morning to match the Blessed Mother's sorrowfulness. Shivering slightly, Mary pulled her handspun mantle a little closer. She took longer pauses at her favourite spots along the Way, feeling a stronger sense of her Son's Presence and a greater need to be with Him on this mournful of mornings. The pull of the wind hampered the gentle Virgin's progress as she struggled up the Hill's gradient so that by the time she had reached its summit, she found herself a little out of breath from the extra exertion. Collapsing to her knees in the soft grass where Jesus had soaked the ground with His Precious Drops of Blood all those years previously, she fell into an ecstasy of prayerful union with her Divine Son.

It is not known the precise circumstances surrounding Mary's death but it stands to good reason that when her time was come, the yearning to be with her Son and its attendant heartache would have become more than her devoted soul could bear. Certainly it can be imagined that this particular morning was just such an occasion. Perhaps once she had reached the summit, the macabre sight of the crucifixions sprinkled along the hilltop brought back more vividly the excruciating agony her Divine Son had endured the day of His Passion, Crucifixion and Death; perhaps there was a Roman crucifixion in progress, the gruesome sound of hammer on nails once again awakening in her soul that torturous pain, like a knife searing into her tender heart. What terrible grieving that Holy Mother must have suffered all those painfully long years without her precious Son. Like any mother mourning the loss of her own child, how much she must have longed to see and to be with Him, remembering all the good times when He would hold her comfortingly in His arms, or look upon her motherly loveliness with such tender love and devotion.

How easily we can now see the Blessed Virgin Mary on her knees in that early morning greyness, the wind moaning all around her in mournful symphony. Who can conjecture how long she may have remained in ecstasy at that holy site, alone in the chilliness of the early misty dawn, unaware of the biting wind tugging all around her and oblivious of the dampness from the fresh dewfall on the wet grass - aware only of the pure joy in her soul in loving communication with God.

No doubt it would have been her beloved John, adopted son chosen by Jesus, with perhaps a few of the other Apostles and Holy Women, who would have come looking for the gentle Virgin, anxious and concerned that she had not appeared that morning to help with the first meal of the day as had been her loving habit so to do. They would have found her slight form prostrate over that sacred site upon the hilltop under the dismal clouds of that cold bleak dawning, a look of pure joy and serenity upon her ethereal countenance. In that instant they would have known the Divine Son had come for His beloved Mother in this her favourite quiet hour of the day, summoning her wholly pure and sweet soul into the joyous bosom of His Father's Kingdom.

Tenderly they would have carried her lifeless body down the hillside, back along the Way of the Cross, to their home in Jerusalem, each and every one of them heartbroken and weeping. How much they would miss the gentle Virgin, for her presence was like an ever-burning flame of love, patience, strength, and gentleness, enkindling their hearts and inspiring them to follow her holy example. Her lovely face and gentle smile were like a light in the darkness to all who were sick or ailing, and her tender words of kindness brought comfort to those who were mourning or in need of consolation, and wisdom to those seeking to know more about her Divine Son and His teachings. It could be said that the very Light of Christ shone through her dark luminous eyes, adding a joyous radiance to her exquisitely serene and lovely countenance.

Many years after her burial, when the tomb was re-opened it was found to be empty.[1] When her earthly life was over, it stands to perfect reason that the Blessed Virgin Mary, immaculate and holy Mother of Jesus, was assumed into Heaven, her body and soul taken up into the Heavenly Kingdom of God.[2] For there was no human soul upon the earth more pure and spotless, not only in her thoughts, words and deeds but also in her pure love of the Triune Godhead.

Dear Mary, Mother of God,
May I be inspired and guided by your holy example
to follow in your Motherly footsteps,
seeking always your loving Help and Intercession.

---

[1] St. Juvenal, Bishop of Jerusalem, at the Council of Chalcedon (451)
[2] Bull Munificentissimus Deus, 1 November, 1950, Pope Pius XII (n. 59)

Chapter 20

A Crown of Glory

Who can imagine the munificence of the Kingdom of Heaven where reigns the All Holy and Most Glorious Beatific Vision of the Almighty Triune God - Father, Son and Holy Ghost - pavilioned in splendour and girded with praise.

Tradition dictates that God is surrounded by angels, being pure spirits created by God, and consisting of nine Choirs or Orders: Seraphim, Cherubim, Thrones, Dominations, Virtues, Powers, Principalities, Archangels and Angels,[1] all praising God on high and giving Him glory and honour for ever more, their melodious strains being more beautiful and unsurpassed by anything ever heard on this earth. We also know from the Transfiguration that God is illuminated by the Light of His pure Love and Divinity, and from the Apocalyptic writings, that *having the glory of God, the light thereof was like to a precious stone, as to the jasper stone, even as crystal.*[2] All who reach the Kingdom of Heaven and abide with God are therefore illuminated by the brilliant Light of His pure Love. The First Epistle of Saint John in holy Scriptures writes, *"Dearly beloved, we are now the sons of God; and it has not yet appeared what we shall be. We know, that, when He appears, we shall be like to Him: because we shall see Him as He is."*[3]

Although *eye has not seen, nor ear heard, neither has it entered into the heart of man, what things God has prepared for those who love Him*[4] we do know that to be with God must be indescribable bliss, for He is infinite Love and Goodness, infinite Peace, infinite Joy, infinite Happiness; all things that the

---

[1] Colossians 1:16
[2] Apocalypse 21:11
[3] 1 John 3:2
[4] 1 Corinthians 2:9

human soul craves on this earth. To be with God would be the ultimate experience, one that we, as pilgrims of this life, should long for and strive to attain.

The path to Heaven is clearly mapped out in holy Scriptures:

> *You shall keep the commandments of the Lord thy God, and walk in His ways, and fear Him;*[5]
>
> *Christ is our advocate. We must keep His commandments and love one another. We must not love the world nor give ear to new teachers, but abide by the spirit of God in His holy Church;*[6]
>
> *Know that the Lord thy God is a strong and faithful God, keeping His covenant and mercy to those who love Him, and to those who keep His commandments;*[7]
>
> *You know the commandments: Honour the Lord they God; Take not the Lord's name in vain; Observe the Sabbath day; Honour thy father and mother; Do not kill; Do not commit adultery; Do not steal; Bear not false witness; Covet not thy neighbour's wife, and nor thy neighbour's goods*[8]

and more importantly through the words of Jesus Christ Himself: *"I say to you, unless a man be born again of water and the Holy Ghost, he cannot enter into the Kingdom of God."*[9] and *"If you keep my commandments, you will abide in my love; as I also have kept my Father's commandments, and do abide in His love"*.[10]

The lowly Virgin Mary certainly aspired to all these things, keeping herself pure of body, heart, mind and soul out of her

---

[5] Deuteronomy 8:6
[6] 1 John 2
[7] Deuteronomy 7:9
[8] Deuteronomy 5:15-21; Mark 10:19
[9] John 3:3 and 5
[10] John 15:10

great love for God. In recognition of her state of holiness and the fact that she had been endowed with the supernatural gift of God's graces, the Archangel Gabriel had hailed her as *Full of Grace*[11] and had called her *Blessed art thou among women;*[12] this wholly pure and saintly virgin, specially chosen by God to conceive miraculously, through the power of the Holy Ghost, the Son of God made man.[13] What great love God must have had for this gentle Maiden to bestow upon her such a powerful and immeasurable honour - to thus become the Mother of our Saviour, Mother of our Redeemer.[14]

And in her role as Mother of the Redeemer, Mary certainly participated in the redemptive mission of her Son Incarnate, not only through her willing *Fiat* in response to the angel's message, wherein she freely cooperated in giving the Second Person of the Holy Trinity His human body, the very instrument of our redemption, but also through her great suffering which was wholly united with that of her Son. Thus it can be said that Mary played a definite role in our salvation - albeit her role one entirely subordinate and dependent on our Lord Jesus Christ. By her free consent to collaborate in God's saving plan, she became our Co-Redemptrix, and, through her close union with the Holy Ghost, our Mediatrix to Jesus (who is the prime Mediator), and also the Advocate for all Christians.[15]

It therefore stands to good reason that Mary, most favoured Lady throughout the universe, would have been gloriously and joyfully welcomed into the Kingdom of Heaven with enormous rejoicing and no doubt a great fanfare of trumpets; imagine the immeasurable joy of the humble Virgin when she came into the omnipotent Presence of her Divine Triune God. Her whole

---

[11] Luke 1:28
[12] Luke 1:28
[13] Luke 1:31-33; Matt. 1:18; Matt. 1:20-23
[14] *Textbooks, CCC, No. 495*
[15] Salvifici Doloris, n.25 (Pope John Paul II), Rosary Encyclicals (Pope Leo XIII), St. Irenaeus (circa 194)

being had been committed to God since birth and throughout her adult life she had remained faithful to her espoused Holy Ghost, a dedicated daughter of the Eternal Father, and devoted Mother to the Son Incarnate, longing for the day when she would reach the Kingdom of Heaven and be united with her beloved Holy Trinity. What a great rejoicing that day; how the Heavens must have resounded with joyous greeting as the Heavenly throng welcomed the Blessed Virgin Mary!

It also stands to reason that the Triune Godhead would have reserved the very highest of places in the Kingdom of Heaven for that lowly and gentle Maiden. The Book of Genesis quotes God's promise to the serpent (the devil) who deceived Adam and Eve at the beginning of Creation that He would *put enmities between you and the Woman, and your seed and her seed: she will crush your head, and you will lie in wait for her heel* [16] For God to grant such powers to such a woman, the Woman would indeed hold a high place in Heaven. Such a Woman would also have to be one whom the sin of Adam and Eve had never tainted, one who was purity itself, just as the bearer of the Christ Child would have had to be purity itself in order to bear the Son of God. The Woman referred to in the Book of Genesis would unquestionably be the Blessed Virgin Mary.

Furthermore, Apocalyptic Scriptures tell of *a great sign that appeared in Heaven: A Woman clothed with the sun, and the moon under her feet, and on her head a crown of twelve stars.* [17] The twelve stars have typically been depicted in holy Scriptures as the twelve Tribes of Abraham, the Israelite.[18] Mary was of the House of David, one of the Tribes of Abraham; and the generation of Jesus Christ accordingly outlined in Matthew's

---

[16] Genesis, Ch.3, v.15
[17] Apocalypse 12:1
[18] Exodus 28:21

Gospel.[19] We therefore see the Blessed Virgin crowned as Queen in the Kingdom of Heaven.

We also know that Jesus found pleasure in granting His Blessed Mother's requests, and that she would gladly intercede on behalf of those in trouble to beg such favours of her Incarnate Son.[20] The road to Heaven being paved with life's challenges and difficulties, let us therefore come to the Blessed Mother of the Son of God with our woes and troubles for her to intercede on our behalf.

For in His last dying moments on the Cross, knowing that John was not Mary's natural son but rather a representative of all mankind, Jesus gave the clear instruction: *"Behold, thy Mother"*, thereby granting His Mother to the whole human race as their supernatural and spiritual Mother. What great love Jesus has for us! He not only gave His life for us, shed all of His Most Precious Blood for us, gives us salvation and eternal life, and a share in His divine nature[21] - but, as if all that weren't enough, He also gives us His own Mother, this beautiful, holy woman that God created to be His Mother, so that we may know and share in the motherly love He put in her heart and turn to her with our urgent supplications to intercede to the Son of God on our behalf.

Dear Mary, Queen of Heaven,
May I be inspired and guided by your holy example
to persevere in Grace and to obtain a crown of Glory hereafter.

---

[19] Matt. 1:1
[20] John 2:4-5
[21] II Peter 1:4

* * * * * * * * *

Remember O most loving Virgin Mary,
that it is a thing unheard of – that anyone who ever had
recourse to thy protection,
implored thy help or sought thine intercession,
was left forsaken.
Filled therefore with confidence in thy goodness,
I fly unto thee O Mother, Virgin of Virgins
To thee do I come,
Before thee do I stand,
a poor sorrowful sinner.
Despise not my poor words, O Holy Mother of the Word of God,
but graciously hear and grant my prayer.
Amen

Hail Mary, full of Grace,
the Lord is with thee.
Blessed art thou among women
and blessed is the Fruit of thy womb, Jesus.
Holy Mary, Mother of God,
Pray for us sinners now
And at the hour of our death.
Amen

* * * * * * * * *

My grateful thanks to:

Rev. Johann G. Roten, SM,
The Marian Library/International Marian Research Institute
and
Rev. Fr. Emanuel Herkel, SSPX

*for taking the time to review my humble work
and for their kind advices to ensure its accuracy*

and to

Jacqueline Haag, Mother's House Publishing
for taking the bold step to publish this, my first writing

Author

As a Source of Comfort to Those Afflicted by Pain and Heartache

This is a story of Love – the pure love of a Mother, who, in the face of terrible hardship and danger, and inconsolable sorrowing, found God's strength and courage to uphold and sustain her, guiding her safely along the path of her sacrificial martyrdom. It is the story of Mary, Blessed Mother of God.

This gentle and lowly Maiden, born of loving yet elderly parents, and brought up in the safe confines of the holy Temple of Jerusalem, was chosen by God to become the Mother of the Redeemer of the whole human race, to bear the torture of her Incarnate Son who gave up His life and abominable sufferings in order to free the human race of their sinfulness and re-open for them the gates of Heaven. No imagination could conjure up the intensity of her great anguish and agony as she bore Christ's afflictions and grievous death on His ignominious cross of crucifixion.

May *The Story of Mary – Mother of Love* reach out and guide the Reader to find a treasury of spiritual gifts to assist and guide their pilgrimage along life's arduous journey toward Heaven, our eternal goal.

As a Devotional Piece

"The Story of Mary – Mother of Love" identifies the Seven Sorrowful Tears and Dolores of the Blessed Virgin Mary, Mother of God, and gently leads the Reader through the fifteen Mysteries of our Redemption - firing the imagination so that one may more readily become caught up in the magic of those Joyous and Glorious Mysteries to be marveled at, or share in the more emotional moments of those Sorrowful Mysteries surrounding the Passion, Crucifixion and Death of our loving Saviour - thereby encouraging meditative prayer, and inspiring the reader to a deeper spiritual devotion to God through the Immaculate Heart of Mary.

Each chapter ends in a prayer, accenting on the virtues of Our Mother in the particular instances of the chapter, to assist in spiritual growth.

As an Educational Tool

"The Story of Mary – Mother of Love" provides the Reader with a simple and enjoyable journey through the four Holy Gospels of the Bible, accenting on the important role the Blessed Virgin Mary, Mother of God, played in the life and times of Jesus Christ, our Redeemer.

Its simple approach should appeal to all age-groups - children and adults - to Christians and non-Christians alike, and provide an easy-to-understand outline of these Holy Scriptures, promoting a better understanding of the importance of Christ in our lives, the great gift of His Redemption, and the wondrous assistance He gave to all of mankind - the gift of His Mother to intercede on our behalf so that we may be helped and guided along life's arduous journey to Heaven, our true home.

Author's Biography

Born into a Protestant family in the mid-forties, London, England, the author met and married the love of her life, a devout Catholic - who brought her to the Blessed Virgin Mary through his own deep devotion. As a couple, with a young family, they traveled across Europe, Africa, and in later years, Canada, their years of traveling providing a wealth of experience, a life filled with excitement, adventure, challenges - inevitable hardship too, to include the tragic death of their baby son. Through it all, they found a deepening faith, an inner strength, courage to face adversity - the joy of life itself, and peace -- the helping hand of a Force far greater than the continents they traversed -- the Hand of Almighty God.

TABLE OF CONTENTS